I0800371

COLUMBUS, INDIANA'S

HISTORIC CRUMP THEATRE

COLUMBUS, INDIANA'S
HISTORIC CRUMP THEATRE

DAVID SECHREST

THE History PRESS

Published by The History Press
Charleston, SC 29403
www.historypress.net

Front cover: Photo by David Williams.

First published 2013

Manufactured in the United States

ISBN 978.1.62619.188.4

Library of Congress CIP data applied for.

A portion of the proceeds from sales of this book will support the Crump Theatre through the Heritage Fund: The Community Foundation of Bartholomew County, Indiana.

For Jennifer, Matthew and Samantha Sechrest.
My world would be so empty without you in my life.

CONTENTS

FOREWORD

Since its beginning as an opera house in the late 1800s, the Crump Theatre has been a landmark in downtown Columbus that has added to our city's cultural offerings. The venerable theater has housed everything from live theatrical performances, silent films and motion pictures to ceremonies, benefits, musical performances and concerts. With its Art Deco façade and large neon marquee lighting up the night sky, the Crump provides a distinct flavor to our city's architectural landscape and urban atmosphere. In 1982, the Crump earned the honor of being placed on the National Register of Historic Places as part of the Columbus Historic District. Rooted deep in Columbus history, our community has developed a strong emotional bond with this historic theater.

The Crump has undergone several extensive renovations during its lifetime, and the strong feelings our community has for this building have also saved it from the wrecking ball. When the Crump seemed doomed for demolition in the late 1980s, our residents stepped up to "Save the Crump"—a movement to restore the theater.

Many significant efforts have gone into reviving the Crump. Over the years, the front façade has been restored, a new marquee has been added, the building's roof has been replaced and many other repairs have been completed. After more than 120 years, we believe the Crump still has plenty of life left in it.

Today, the Crump is one of the many assets that adds to the newly developed Columbus Arts District. It stands as a testament to our community's desire to preserve history. We are hopeful the Crump can return as a cultural magnet in our community and become economically vital once again.

In this book, author and historian David Sechrest provides a historical narrative of the Crump covering a time period from 1872 to the present day. He gives in-depth perspective to the importance of the Crump in Columbus and shows how the theater's long history has endeared it to so many in our community.

The future of the Crump is bright with potential. Please take time to appreciate its history, and thank you for your contribution to its future through the purchase of this book.

—Mayor Kristen Brown

ACKNOWLEDGEMENTS

So many people helped in guiding me along this path of discovery. I want to thank:

Mayor Kristen Brown for writing the foreword to this book.

Everyone at the Bartholomew County Historical Society and especially Nick Speth for his assistance in locating photographs for this book. Also, thanks to the staff at the Bartholomew County Public Library, in particular, Tyler Munn, for his assistance in getting microfilm copies of the *Big Blue Union* newspaper (Marysville, Kansas) so quickly. Thanks also to the people at the Marysville, Kansas Historical Society.

A sincere thank-you to Rovene Quigley for allowing me to put this book's title on the Crump Theatre marquee.

Thanks to Dan Patterson for allowing me to see and photograph his original Crump Theatre chair. Thanks to my dear friend Jack Fitzpatrick for helping to date the chair and for his assistance with the Crump Theatre marquee lettering.

Thanks to Bob Anderson, Stillframes Photography, for all the wonderful pictures he took of the Crump Theatre. Also, thank you for digitizing the negatives and slides for use in this book.

Acknowledgements

A big thank-you to Randy Weinantz for loaning me his mother, Joan's, scrapbook. The information your mother compiled was of tremendous benefit, but more than that, it was what started me on this journey ten years ago.

Thanks to Tamara Stone Iorio for letting me include images from her wonderful postcard collection and to Carol Ahlbrand for the pictures of her grandfather, Walter Doup.

A sincere thank-you to Francis Jefferson Crump III, Rovene Quigley, Christine Lemley, Ed Sullivan, Vernon Jewell, Jayne Farber, Henry Malm, Hutch Schumaker, Louis Joyner, Michael Rembusch and Trudie Schoettmer for taking time away from their busy schedules to talk with me about the Crump Theatre. (One of these days, I'll get this interview thing down pat!)

Thanks to Lesley Carter and Joy Sechrest Brown for their beautiful, original pieces of artwork. This book would not be the same without your artistic offerings.

And last but by no means least, a sincere thank-you to Herschel Crippen Jr., Rick Weinantz, Connie Weinantz Jeesse, Abby Abel McGovern, Gary Scroggins, David Yount and Harry McCawley.

PART 1

THE ROAD TO SUCCESS IS PAVED WITH FAILURE (COLUMBUS, INDIANA OPERA HOUSES AND THEATERS, 1872–89)

1872
F.J. CRUMP'S OPERA HOUSE

A Place of Which No Citizen Should Feel Ashamed

The Crump Theatre will celebrate its 124th birthday on October 30, 2013. The building that will celebrate this historic anniversary is actually a combination of two buildings: Keith's Arcade, which was built in 1871, and the theater building that architect Charles Sparrell designed and contractors Keller and Brockman adjoined to the back of the Arcade building. When Crump's New Theatre first opened on that rainy Wednesday night of October 30, 1889, a milestone in the field of dramatic arts was finally achieved. It had taken more than seventeen years to get to that place in time. The years leading up to the opening of Crump's New Theatre were littered with catastrophic failures, coupled with a small degree of success. All that had transpired had been a costly learning curve. This narrative does not begin on that opening night, for to truly appreciate the importance of Columbus, Indiana's first successful venue for the cultural arts, it is necessary to backtrack and start at the beginning.

This is what happened. This is my attempt at squeezing those 124 years into a forty-thousand-word book.

In 1872, the population of Columbus Township was roughly 3,350 people. The town of Columbus proper spread itself out over a seventy-block area, from Water Street at the south up to North Street (Tenth) and from Brown Street on the west to Wilson. The town was a mish-mash of homes and churches; merchants and banks; woolen mills and meat-processing plants; grain, grist- and feed mills; livery stables and boardinghouses; wagon makers; furniture builders; and undertakers. Railroad Square occupied an entire block in the heart of downtown. Sanitary conditions were poor. Drainage ditches were dug by hand along the sides of dirt streets, some doing nothing more than offering a place for stagnant water to pond up. The intersection of Walnut (Fourth) and Franklin Streets got so bad after a heavy rain that it was nicknamed Storey Lake, as water levels were more than knee high. Dead pigs, dogs, cats and rats were a common sight (and smell) in alleyways. Cattle, turkeys, sheep and pigs were herded along Washington Street and could be seen wandering the downtown streets of their own free will.

Despite the town's shortcomings, the residents of Columbus took much pride in their city. Exciting things were happening. P.H. McCormack and P.H. Sweeney were building a magnificent new courthouse at the southwest corner of Tipton (Third) and Washington Streets. During the first six months of 1872 alone, directors of the Jeffersonville, Madison and Indianapolis Railroad came to town to discuss plans for a new hotel and larger depot; Harry Frantz was busy fitting up his new soda fountain (the town's first) on Washington Street; and R.M. Darnell opened his Palace of Fashion inside the Keith's Arcade building on Tipton (Third) Street.

Something even more exciting was taking place at the northeast corner of Walnut (Fourth) and Washington Streets—Francis Jefferson Crump's Opera House was under construction. It would be a vast improvement over Keith's Opera Hall above Isham Keith's Hardware at the corner of Tipton (Third) and Washington Streets, and to the residents of Columbus, a new opera house was desperately needed. The town offered great opportunities for outside capitalists interested in moving here. There were good schools, clubs to fraternize and a variety of churches to attend. But the one thing Columbus sorely lacked was an ample place for the performing arts. Hopefully, F.J. Crump's Opera House would fulfill this desire. An actual opera house would announce that Columbus offered the best of everything. Quite possibly, it was also a necessary evil in the mind of F.J. Crump. Such a thought most likely crossed his mind on more than one occasion.

Francis Crump was seventy-one years old. He had watched Columbus grow from nothing more than a virgin forest, having participated in the town's birth and its constant struggles along the way. He was twenty years old when he first stepped foot onto Bartholomew County soil. That long journey from Virginia closed one chapter in his life, and as he jumped down from that spring wagon and first set foot on Bartholomew County soil in early 1821, another chapter immediately got underway.

Francis Jefferson Crump was born in Niggerfoot, Virginia, on January 31, 1801. At a young age, he was bound out to Thomas Wood and learned the carpenter and wood-joiner trade. There are differing accounts regarding his departure from home. One version follows that he ran away from Thomas Wood, while another suggests that he and his father were in strong disagreement regarding the issue of slavery. Nonetheless, during his late teens, he either ran away or simply left home. Possibly in Bowling Green, Virginia, he hooked up with Burl Glanton and his family. The Glantons were headed west to the New Territory, and Francis joined up with them, driving one of Glanton's spring wagons. They traveled across the mountains of West Virginia, across the hilly Kentucky countryside, most likely headed north to Madison, Indiana, upon reaching Lexington, Kentucky, and arrived in Columbus in early 1821. That day he first stepped foot onto Bartholomew County soil, it is said he had fifty cents in his pocket.

On his arrival, Francis and his carpentry skills were put to good use. Sickness and disease were so prevalent that the first year he was kept busy building coffins. It is unknown whether Francis helped to erect the town's first courthouse (present site today), but he and Burl Glanton did build the town's first merchant district: the Orr Corner (possibly the west or south side of our present-day courthouse). In 1826, at the age of twenty-five, he married Emilia Smith. Together, they helped found the first Christian church in Columbus.

To gaze upon Francis was to look upon a giant of a man. He stood six feet, four inches tall on a slim, muscular frame. To add to his height, he wore a tall stovepipe hat, giving him the appearance of being close to seven feet tall. His eyes were dark, deep and penetrating; his facial features were those of a man who took life seriously. But within the eyes and stern features was also a look of compassion for his fellow man.

Land patents show that Francis bought land in October 1834, acquiring a 40-acre tract north and west of town (vicinity of today's Everroad Park). On September 21, 1835, he added to his property holdings and bought 120 acres farther west of town (north of present-day Sand Hill Cemetery). But Francis Jefferson Crump III shared with me that his great-great grandfather first bought property in Bartholomew County in 1826. This property was two miles north of Columbus city limits at the time (vicinity of present-day Mead Village) and would become known as the Crump Homestead. In 1846, Emilia died, leaving Francis with six children to raise on his own. After Emilia's death, the family continued to live on the Crump Homestead until 1854, when they moved into town and took up residence in a two-story house on the north side of Walnut (Fourth) Street (vicinity of today's Smith's Row).

Francis Jefferson Crump. *Courtesy of Francis Jefferson Crump III.*

From the time of his arrival, Francis managed to put back a fair amount of money, and around 1831, he began lending money. He saw no need for an office and carried his notes and important papers in his stovepipe hat. In 1849, he took out an ad in the *Weekly Democrat* newspaper: "Francis J. Crump, Note Broker, Office in His Hat." By 1865, Francis and Randolph Griffith, along with eight other capitalists, formed the First National Bank.

Francis Crump was a self-made man. His was the typical rags-to-riches story of a select few of our pioneering forefathers. Through hard work, wise investments and real estate ventures, he became one of the wealthiest men in not only in the town of Columbus but also in the state of Indiana.

Francis Crump's Opera House was not a "stand-alone" place for amusements. Rather, the first floor consisted of rooms for four businesses, with the actual opera hall on the second floor. By June 1872, work on the first floor was completed. The first merchant to occupy one of the four available rooms was bookseller John B. Cobb (in 1865, Cobb opened the first bookstore in Columbus). The first amusement held at Crump's was a Strawberry Festival, hosted by the women of the M.E. Church on Tuesday, June 4, 1872, while the building was still under construction.

Work progressed on the opera hall through the summer months. It is unknown who F.J. Crump hired to build the two-story brick building, but by July, Hege and Mathes, local contractors, undertook the job of providing woodwork for the second-floor opera hall. In late August, Francis employed Indianapolis artist Julien G. Reynolds to paint the numerous scenes that would be used to provide the backdrops for stage plays, as well as advertisements on the thirteen-and-a-half- by twenty-four-and-a-half-foot drop curtain. These business cards were two feet by three feet and advertised the services of local merchants that bought space. Julien also frescoed the ceiling.

F.J. Crump's Opera House opened to a packed house on Monday evening, October 21, 1872. The White and Turner Troupe performed *The Poor Girl's Diary* and a comedy. The following evening, the troupe presented *Under the Gas Light*. One of the more popular members of the troupe was Miss Emma Leland. A special benefit for her was called out by patrons, and more than one hundred signatures requesting such were given to her. The benefit in her honor was held on Monday, October 28, 1872, and was followed by a benefit for Mr. White the following evening. By Wednesday morning, the troupe boarded a train for Barrett's Theater in New Orleans. They would not return to Crump's Opera House.

Days before the opening, on Thursday, October 17, 1872, the *Columbus Republican* newspaper had this to say about Crump's hall: "Columbus has now a hall of which none of her citizens need to be ashamed, though it is much regretted that Mr. Crump did not build it a little more in the style of an opera house."

There had been one other so-called opera house in Columbus prior to the opening of Crump's. Keith's Hall, on the second story of Keith's Building, was situated at the southeast corner of Tipton (Third) and Washington Streets. It was noted as an "Opera House" in *Columbus Republican* newspaper advertisements. In tracing back the history of local places of amusements,

An artistic interpretation of what F.J. Crump's Opera House may have looked like. *Drawing by Joy Sechrest Brown.*

Keith's might have been the first, although it is not known what year it opened. But Keith's Hall wasn't really an opera hall—at least not in the minds of the theatergoing public. It was much too small to accommodate the needs of the prominent traveling shows of the day. Crump's Opera Hall was larger than Keith's, and once inside, it gave the appearance of what the theatergoing public perceived as close to a true opera hall as could be expected in the small town of Columbus. Because Crump's offered more space than Keith's Hall, larger, more prestigious traveling shows of the day could be booked during the opera season. Crump's Opera House was also used for local dances, balls, socials and dramatic club amusements. As a final note here, with the opening of Crump's Opera Hall, Keith's Hall would never again be used as a venue for the theater arts. Up until the time the building was demolished in 1882, it was used for dances and balls.

In conjunction with the building of Crump's Opera House, a group of unnamed capitalists formed the Columbus Lecture Association in June 1872. Its purpose was to provide the residents of Bartholomew County and southern Indiana with prominent, national orators of the day, including Mark Twain, Julia Ward Howe, James E. Murdoch and Frederick Douglass.

Twain, Howe and Murdoch never appeared on stage at Crump's Opera House, but Frederick Douglass did. Douglass arrived in Columbus on Monday, January 6, 1873, for a one-evening engagement. He was scheduled to speak on the subject of the "Self Made Man," but upon taking the stage, he informed the audience that he could not present that particular topic, for he had lost all his papers when his Rochester, New York home was destroyed by fire the year before. Instead, he spoke of the antislavery movement, the future of the country and the equality of the races. He was paid one hundred dollars for the engagement.

Editors of the *Columbus Republican* newspaper were none too happy with the turnout for such a revered speaker of the day:

> *The people of Columbus do themselves an honor of a questionable nature when they express their preference of a minstrel show to an intellectual entertainment in as emphatic a manner as they have done this winter. The question of the comparative popularity of mock negroes without brains and a real negro with brains has been fairly tried, and the decision has been given in favor of the former, with a majority of almost two to one. Cal. Wagner, with his dozen artists in burnt cork, can draw a crowded house and carry away two hundred and sixteen dollars tribute from our citizens to his hackneyed nonsense, but the Lecture Association may bring one of the most celebrated orators of the time, and they will barely pay expenses. In view of this marked taste for tomfoolery and the distaste for intellectual things on the part of the community, the suggestion has been made to the lecture committee to introduce the remainder of the lecturers in the character of plantation negroes and instruct them to substitute grimaces for humor, stale jokes for wit, conundrums for logic and song and dance for eloquence. By these means, our visitor will not be disappointed of getting well-filled houses, a large portion of our people will be entertained with performances which they will appreciate and pronounce capital, and the Lecture Association will be spared the necessity of declaring repealed dividends of assessments in order to pay expenses.*

After expenses, the Columbus Lecture Association realized a net profit of $5.95 from the Douglass speaking engagement. Noted actor James E. Murdoch came very close to performing at Crump's hall but had to cancel at the last minute due to a bout with the flu. His engagement was not rescheduled.

A foretelling of the demise of Crump's hall occurred on the evening of Wednesday, May 14, 1873. Will Carruthers went inside to check on the place and, upon entering the stage area, looked up and saw the proscenium on fire. He was most definitely at the right place and at the right time. If he would have waited another hour, Crump's hall would have been destroyed. The fire was put out with minimal damage. The cause of the blaze was a mystery, as there were no fires in the hall since the day before.

The summer months of 1873 passed quite nicely in Columbus. In mid-June, F.J. Crump put up an iron fence around his Walnut (Fourth) Street home. By the end of July, the roof of his opera house had a fresh coat of paint. The last day of September was a terrible day in Columbus history. A run was made on the First National Bank. For a while, things appeared very bleak. A courier was sent to Cincinnati to secure necessary funds, but none were to be had. It appeared the run on the bank would force it to close its doors. Attending to the moment of crisis, F.J. Crump stepped forth, threw open his huge pocketbook and offered up his own funds to the amount of $100,000 in money and mortgage notes. He was able to quell the crowd and save the economic stability of the First National Bank from one of the nastiest days in Columbus history.

October 1873 found the four business rooms of Crump's Opera House completely filled. J.B. Cobb proudly offered his stationery and books; the Piel Brothers offered groceries and provisions; John Keith and Sons, another grocery store; and the Singer Sewing Machine Company, its sewing wares. Earlier that year, S.J. Harris had relocated his jewelry business from the McEwen Block into a one-story, wood-frame structure directly north of Crump's. Grocers Cooper and Duffy opened a branch store in Harris's new building, and druggists Barret and Hauser rounded out the merchant offerings in the Harris building.

On Thursday evening, October 16, 1873, the Helen D'Este Troupe was busy performing to an enthusiastic crowd at Crump's hall. The troupe had engaged the hall for two weeks, and patrons and newspaper editors alike were thrilled with their performances (newspaper editors were notorious stage critics during this time). Another benefit was called for by the theatergoing crowd, this time to honor Miss D'Este.

It would never take place inside Crump's Opera House.

At 4:00 a.m. on Saturday, October 18, 1873, Will Carruthers was completely oblivious to the scenario unfolding at the corner of Walnut (Fourth) and Washington Streets. He would play no role at Crump's Opera House this time. At approximately 4:20, everyone within bell-ringing and shouting distance was rousted from their beds by shouts of, "Fire!"

Crump's Opera House was ablaze in the chilly, early morning October air.

Shortly before Christmas 1872, Francis Crump employed a young George Pence to rearrange the chairs in the opera hall (Pence would later become Bartholomew County's first historian). He laid them out so everyone would have the best possible view of the stage. His job was two-fold: to rearrange the chairs, and to paint numbers on the reserved seats. The chairs that George Pence had devoted so much time to arranging and numbering were now providing fuel to the growing fire, as were the massive drop curtain and the large canvases that Julien Reynolds had meticulously painted. The intense heat had burned its way through the ceiling. The roof was on fire.

The fire company arrived while Mrs. Cooper and her son, G.W. Cooper, frantically rushed in and out of the S.J. Harris building next door, clearing out all the important papers and provisions they could carry. As hoses were attached to the fire hydrants, Sam Kline climbed up the side of the building that the Coopers were busy racing in and out of and stood on the roof directly above Barret & Hauser Drugs, grasping a fire hose in both hands. Cries went out to increase the steam pressure at the waterworks so that enough pressure could be built up in the water lines to fight the inferno.

The scene unfolding was chaotic. Nothing was going as it should. There was a problem at the waterworks, and the needed steam pressure was too slow in coming. Sam Kline stood helpless on the roof, holding in his hands a fire hose that wouldn't work. He could do no more than the hundreds of bystanders on the street: watch as the horror unfolded.

The fire began to spread. It jumped and arced its way across Walnut (Fourth) Street, and pockets of flames began popping up on the north side of the Griffith Block (First National Bank building). Cries desperately called out for more water pressure.

The Coopers made one final, valiant attempt at saving what they could. They raced into the building, grabbed the money from the cash drawer and hurried out. As they reached the threshold leading onto Washington Street, the north wall and roof of the opera house collapsed, destroying the building the Coopers had just exited. Damage to life and limb had been spared by mere seconds. Seconds before the wall collapsed, Sam Kline threw down the worthless fire hose he held in his hands and jumped onto the Washington Street sidewalk below. He was a little sore, but he was alive. Citizens and fire personnel were now fighting the growing flames across the street. Horrors of the fire spreading from building to building, block to block, crept up in the backs of everyone's mind.

The heat from the opera house fire was so intense that it broke out the glass windows on the north side of the building across Walnut Street (Griffith's Block), and for a while, it appeared the entire downtown could be destroyed. It took forty-five minutes before enough pressure finally built up in the water lines. By that time, it was too late. Crump's Opera House was in ashes.

The fires across the street were eventually extinguished, as was the opera house fire. Damage to Crump's building was costly on both a financial and personal level. J.B. Cobb's losses amounted to $3,200 (insured for $2,000); Piel Brothers, $3,600 (insured for $1,500); and the John Keith & Company, $3,000 (no insurance). Damage at the Singer Sewing Machine Company was estimated between $6,000 and $7,000 (no insurance). S.J. Harris's building next door sustained $800 in damage (insured for $700), while Cooper and Duffy realized a loss of $2,000 (insured for $1,500), due to the falling wall.

But Francis J. Crump suffered the greatest financial loss, as the second story of his building was totally destroyed. The loss amounted to $20,000. To make matters worse, he had no insurance on the building.

The Helen D'Este theatrical troupe also experienced tremendous losses. Helen D'Este lost her entire wardrobe, consisting of 103 dresses that were stored in the hall. Her loss was estimated at $4,600. Probably the most tragic personal loss was that of C. Toyler Wolfe, a member of the troupe. Besides his wardrobe, he lost his handwritten manuscript of a history of the Civil War and an autobiography of his fifty years spent on stage, both close to completion (he was looking for a publisher). Damage across the street at Griffith's Block consisted of $600 to cover broken windows from the intense heat of the opera house fire.

The origin of the Crump Opera House fire was a mystery. Friedgen and Donner, owners of a photography business in Columbus, set up their camera and took pictures of the Crump Opera House ruins later that morning (sadly, none of those images exist today).

The destruction of Crump's Opera House was a terrible blow to the citizens of Columbus. At the time, it was the largest hall in the city. The hall could accommodate 1,000 to 1,200 patrons. It had been built specifically to capitalize on those large crowds, which in turn would help attract the attention of more nationally recognized stage performers of the day to Columbus. Not only had the fire destroyed the Opera House, but it also destroyed the link to a higher class of amusements. Its destruction would hinder any attempts to bring nationally prominent amusements to Columbus.

It is interesting to speculate on such matters as the Crump Opera House fire. What if the building had not been destroyed? What role would its existence have played in the shaping of our present downtown? It is quite possible that corner of Fourth and Washington might look much different today had the fire never happened.

1873

JOHN GEORGE SCHWARTZKOPF'S GERMANIA HALL

A Time of Uncertainty

Later that morning, while the opera house lay in ruin and still smoldering, John G. Schwartzkopf, a prominent Columbus businessman and wagon maker, stepped forward.

In early 1873, a new two-story building for J.G. Schwartzkopf was undertaken by local contractors. This new building was situated on Jackson Street, across from the courthouse. Initially, Schwartzkopf planned for a business on the first floor and a dancing hall on the second. But that morning, in light of the destruction of Crump's Opera House, he quickly changed those plans. With his new two-story building very close to completion, he proposed the second floor be used as an opera hall for the citizens of Columbus. The consensus was both immediate and unanimous. Work began immediately to get the unfinished second story of his building in proper order for a performance later that evening.

With Crump's Opera House smoldering in the early morning light, work commenced to transform the second floor of Schwartzkopf's building from an unfinished hall into an opera house. Plastering of the second-story walls had just been completed, and men went to work installing windows. A temporary stage was thrown up, and chairs were borrowed from Keith's Hall. Schwartzkopf's Hall was half the size of Crump's, providing seating for perhaps five hundred people, but this was not an important issue at the time. The citizens of Columbus were just happy to have another place for amusements, and especially under such quick notice.

Even though they had lost their wardrobes, and no scenery was available, the Helen D'Este theatrical troupe played the Schwartzkopf Opera Hall that Saturday evening, mere hours after the destruction of Crump's Opera House.

J.G. Schwartzkopf named his new hall the Germania.

The question on everyone's mind following the fire was whether F.J. Crump would rebuild his hall? As workmen busied themselves clearing away the rubble, rumors began to circulate that he would not. He would turn the existing structure into a one-story building consisting of nothing more than business rooms. Editors of the *Columbus Republican* were furious with this thought:

> *Men are now at work clearing away the rubbish at the ruins of the Opera House block, but it is rumored that Mr. Crump will not rebuild the hall, and there are only designs to finish the block as one-story business rooms. If this is Mr. Crump's determination, we hope he will reconsider the matter before it is too late. Columbus must have a hall, and no man is more able to build one that he is, and there is no better location in the city than the site of the ruins. Mr. Crump is growing old, and a neat and substantial hall can be built upon the present site which would be of vast importance to the city and a monument to his memory that would last for years after he had passed away. What is gold, locked up in bank vaults, left for children to fight over? A few years, and it will be differently invested, and no monument left to recall the name of him who had toiled through the years of trouble and anxiety to acquire the fortune. Money cannot benefit the dead, nor can it benefit a city, when not invested in improvements that would be a credit and a benefit to all classes. What is a city without a hall? It is like the miser without a name. If men would look at this matter in the proper light, they would readily see the folly of locking up money to leave behind when death knocks at the door. Such a course has been the ruin of thousands of heirs to fortunes, as the ready cash is a temptation to immediate recklessness, when if fortunes are left in valuable property, it is not only a benefit to all in the city or neighborhood where it is located, but is of vast more importance to children to whom it is left, as they will value that property in the same proportion the community values it, and thus the temptation to squander the fortune by the heirs is materially weakened, and the property may thus be a blessing to them when the ready money would be a curse. Chauncy Rose, of Terre Haute, is putting his money into costly buildings which will honor his*

> *name as long as marble and stone last, and those who look upon the beautiful marble fronts erected by him on Main Street will cherish his memory for ages after he has passed away, just because he loved the city and left the proof behind. When a man toils for a lifetime and hoards his wealth away in cash and stocks, not visible to the community he lives in, it seems a virtual admission that he leaves his wealth to those more capable of investing his money than he himself. This is unjust to his memory and cannot be corrected after his death.*

While people and paper speculated on its outcome, J.G. Schwartzkopf was busy with his Germania Hall. He had a partition cut out, thus offering a stage of eighteen feet deep. Permanent chairs were secured, and Schwartzkopf hired local painter Charlie Fowler to begin work on painting the necessary scenery and providing stage artistry. An agent for the Wallace Sisters had engaged Germania Hall for the evening of Wednesday, November 5. The stage would be completed by that time.

Schwartzkopf's Opera House was known by several names: Schwartzkopf's, the Germania and Opera House. By the 1880s, it would simply become known as the Opera House.

The editors of the *Columbus Republican* kept Crump's Opera House in the news. They were absolutely convinced the best thing he could do would be to rebuild. Crump's hall was just days shy of its one-year anniversary. Any profits realized by Francis were most likely minimal. But while calls were made on F.J. Crump's character and his leaving any lasting monument to the city, he remained quiet.

Meanwhile, Charlie Fowler was busy painting scenery for the Germania. By November 20, he had completed nine scenes. Praise was given to his street, garden and fountain scenes as being realistic works. Charlie's talent was also recognized by a group from Richmond, Indiana, and he was hired to decorate and provide scenery for an opera hall in that city as well.

By November 27, work on the Harris building was completed, and it was once again open for business. Cooper & Duffy moved back in a few days later. The Columbus Quadrille Club offered up a grand ball in Germania Hall in early January 1874, and F.J. Crump finally spoke: his old opera house building would be constructed only one story high. Editors at the *Columbus Republican* were none too happy: "We hope Mr. Crump will use his better judgment and not disfigure the business part of our town with such a flat boat." Soon after his announcement, F.J. Crump took sick and confined himself to his home.

By March 1874, Keith's Hall was suddenly going by a new name: Maennerchor Hall. The Columbus Cornet Band offered up a ball there on March 10. It would never function as an opera house again.

By the spring of 1874, F.J. Crump had recovered from his illness and was back at work at the First National Bank. Not only was he back, but news of his opera house—or lack thereof—resurfaced as well. There would be no opera house. The *Columbus Republican* reported:

> *F.J. Crump has recovered from his illness and is now out upon the street attending to business, and he reports that he has contracted to shed over the Opera House corner as a one-story building. This is an insult to the city in which he has made his fortune and to the property holders in the locality, as such a building will be a miserly monument of folly as long as it may stand. A man who is worth from two to three hundred thousand dollars, having no particular use for his money, and not many years to live in this world, and without the last prospect of taking his fortune with him into the next, is certainly imbued with an unnatural grasp on the almighty dollar, to thus bedaub the finest corner in the city. Property holders interested in the building up of this corner offer to make up $1,000 and give it to Mr. C. if he will only consent to rebuild the opera house, which will not cost more than $20,000 extra over and above his present plan, but this has no influence upon his present determination, as one man has said that he would not take a room in the building if the hall was put over it. While one man may have such a notion, hundreds of others would readily give from one to two hundred dollars more rent per year than the rooms in a one-story house would command. These are facts, and we hope Mr. C. will not commit the greatest blunder of his life, just at the close of his eventful career. Such a building as is now contracted for will be an eye-sore as long as it may stand and will depreciate property in the neighborhood 20 percent. Mark these words, and time will prove them true as gospel.*

In his book *I Discover Columbus*, William Marsh wrote that F.J. Crump's response to rebuilding the opera house was along the line of "not until Hell freezes over." He would not be the last to make such a statement.

Thus ends the story of Columbus, Indiana's first actual opera house.

1875

McCORMACK AND SWEENEY'S PALLAS THEATER

A New Beginning

Fast forward to April 1875. Contractors McCormack and Sweeney, whose majestic new courthouse now graced the corner of Tipton (Third) and Washington, have announced the purchase of the Mrs. Young corner at Harrison (Fifth) and Washington Streets. Their intent is to build a block of buildings, and they offer to put up a commodious opera house—but only if the citizens of Columbus agree to purchase $2,500 to $3,000 of stock with a guarantee that all stock options will be bought back after a period of five years. Plans and specifications were made available for public viewing.

Even though their offer was gracious, there seemed no hope of the hall being built, as such philanthropy was a tight commodity. J.G. Schwartzkopf, most likely fed up with the whole mess, announced that if McCormack and Sweeney did not build an opera house, he would add eighty feet to the west end of Germania Hall.

Construction on the McCormack and Sweeney block commenced the last of April 1875. The corner would become known as Builders Hall.

While the two contractors debated over the opera house question, George P. Bissell paid a visit to Columbus. Bissell had traveled from New York City to arrange for the conversion of the old McEwen block into a first-class hotel for the city. The contract for renovating the property was let on April 27, 1875, to Roger Bowley & Co. for $7, 985, with plans to open the hotel in September.

It is unknown where the money came from or any of the details regarding McCormack and Sweeney's decision to build an opera hall, but by the end of July, their decision was made. The theatergoing members of the community were excited about the upcoming opera season. The new McCormack & Sweeney Opera House would be the place offering such entertainment. It would be larger than the Germania and would offer two galleries, private boxes and a seating capacity of roughly 1,200. It would be comparable in size to F.J. Crump's Opera House.

In August, trees were cut down, exposing the front along Washington Street. In early September, work began on the roof. While doing work at the top of the north wall, brick mason Frank Uberroth Sr. accidentally stepped on a layer of freshly laid brick. The brick gave way, and Frank fell forty feet to the pavement below. He died half an hour after the fall. Morris Spinner fell from a scaffold attached to the opera house around the same time, suffering only a broken leg. On September 9, the suggestion was made to hold a concert for the benefit of McCormack and Sweeney on Opening Day. J.B. Cobb, now relocated back at Crump's Block "flat boat" building, had expanded his book and stationery business to include musical instruments and had taken on a partner, Mr. Hutchins. They proposed offering their pianos and organs for the occasion.

Across town at the old McEwen Block, the hotel was coming along just fine. Ironwork for the veranda was up, and opening day for Columbus's new hotel wasn't far off. It now had a name: the Bissell Hotel.

On Friday evening, October 29, 1875, McCormack and Sweeney's Pallas Theater was dedicated. The event was by invitation only, with tickets costing a whopping $2 per person. A dance was held, and approximately sixty couples attended the grand occasion. The front of the Pallas Theater held nine lights of glass measuring fifty-two and a half inches by eighty-four inches. The glass was made at the New Albany Glass Works at a cost of $486. By December, eighteen pieces of stone, each twelve feet in length, were laid in front of the Pallas.

The Pallas Theater was laid out in similar style to Crump's. The first floor housed businesses, while the theater was located on the second floor. The first to occupy a place of business on the first floor was Smith & Henderson, newcomers to Columbus and dealers in fine caps, shoes, hats and boots.

Roughly two months later, at nine o'clock on Friday evening, December 17, the Bissell Hotel was officially opened at the northwest corner of Tipton (Third) and Franklin Streets. More than two hundred persons attended the celebratory dinner and ball. Now Columbus would offer both a wonderful theater and a first-class hotel to accommodate traveling shows.

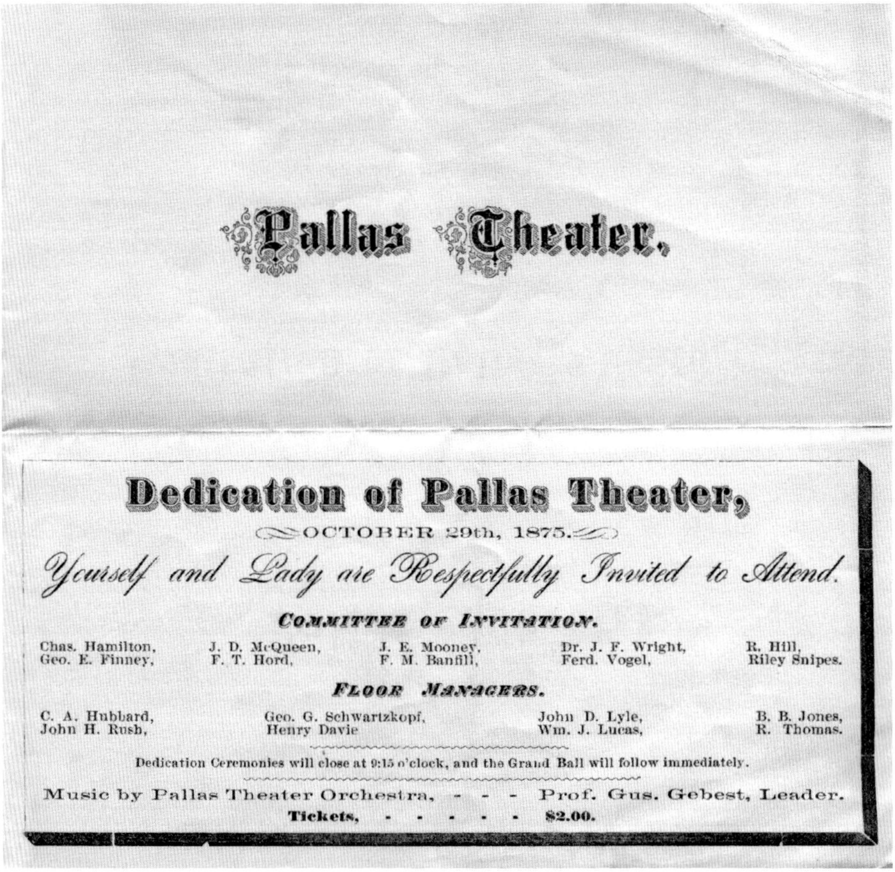

Pallas Theater.

Dedication of Pallas Theater,

OCTOBER 29th, 1875.

Yourself and Lady are Respectfully Invited to Attend.

COMMITTEE OF INVITATION.

Chas. Hamilton,	J. D. McQueen,	J. E. Mooney,	Dr. J. F. Wright,	R. Hill,
Geo. E. Finney,	F. T. Hord,	F. M. Banfill,	Ferd. Vogel,	Riley Snipes.

FLOOR MANAGERS.

C. A. Hubbard,	Geo. G. Schwartzkopf,	John D. Lyle,	B. B. Jones,
John H. Rush,	Henry Davie	Wm. J. Lucas,	R. Thomas.

Dedication Ceremonies will close at 9:15 o'clock, and the Grand Ball will follow immediately.

Music by Pallas Theater Orchestra, - - - Prof. Gus. Gebest, Leader.

Tickets, - - - - - - $2.00.

Invitation for the dedication of McCormack and Sweeney's Pallas Theater, October 29, 1875. *Author's collection.*

The New Year of 1876 was celebrated exuberantly by townspeople. At midnight, every bell in the city was sounded, anvils were fired and people marched through the streets. Some residents thought the city was on fire. In February, A.P. Warner opened his Pallas Grocery underneath the Pallas Theater. Dr. Ball's Cough Syrup was just the ticket to cure those late-night theatergoers from coughs or cold. Mr. DeLang arrived from Evansville and rented a room underneath the Pallas for the purpose of selling jewelry. The Parlor Jewelry Store would officially open on Monday, March 13. And to complete the downstairs business picture, the Singer Sewing Machine Company relocated underneath the theater that same month.

The Pallas slowly gained the national recognition that Crump's Opera Hall had briefly touched upon. Troupes and acts were booked from all over the country. And over the next few years, the city of Columbus continued to prosper, the *Republican* editors continued to complain and fires continued to be a nuisance.

1879–80

PALLAS THEATER FIRE, SCHWARTZKOPF'S HALL REMODELED AND THE THIRD STREET VARIETY THEATER

Jump to 1879. On Thursday, February 20, bills were put up around town announcing the Original New Orleans Minstrels' appearance at the Pallas Theater the following Tuesday, February 25. Also appearing on the bill was Gorton's Gold Band, Russian athletes and twenty first-class artists—all for the mere price of thirty-five or fifty cents. Businesses located underneath the theater now consisted of Howard Duffy (half of Cooper & Duffy) and his grocery business; Lee Joseph, dealer in dry goods; S.S. Carruthers, furniture; and Joseph Varner's restaurant. Joseph lived in the rear part of the restaurant.

Slightly past 1:00 a.m. on February 20, Joseph Varner was awakened by the sound of something falling over. The sound came from Carruthers's adjoining furniture store. Varner got up, got dressed and stepped outside the back door. That's when he saw the flames leaping from inside Carruthers's furniture room. Immediately, he sounded the alarm, bringing night policeman Newt Bryant to the scene. The fire bell was sounded, and fire chief H.C. Davie arrived on the scene, quickly followed by his men. Due to the fuel the furniture provided, it didn't take the fire long before it had burned through the ceiling and up the walls, setting the upstairs theater ablaze. The fire spread rapidly throughout the theater, setting the interior of the roof ablaze. The intensity of the fire suddenly shifted from the first floor to the second. Dense smoke poured from the crevices, doorways and windows of the first floor, hampering any attempt to battle the blaze from inside. To make matters worse, the tin roof acted as a barrier and kept any directed streams of water from reaching the interior ceiling of the theater. With the firemen busy, Varner removed as much furniture from his restaurant as he could. Howard Duffy, who appeared on the scene around the same time as Chief Davie, was busy removing all he could carry from his grocery business. With the assistance of others, he was able to save much of his inventory. Carruthers wasn't as lucky. Most of his inventory was destroyed, as was Lee Joseph's dry goods stock.

As with Crump's Opera House, the cause of the fire remained a mystery. Thankfully, there were no lives lost. Most losses by all parties were partially insured. The greatest loss to the merchants would be the time incurred in relocating their wares. McCormack and Sweeney estimated the value of the Pallas Theater building at $35,000. Their insurance (through six different companies) amounted to $10,375. The exterior brick walls were all found to be sound, with the exception of the west side, which would need to be rebuilt. As for the Original New Orleans Minstrels, the show was relocated to Germania Hall and at the last minute was changed to the old Christian church.

While McCormack and Sweeney worked with their respective insurance companies, they accepted bids for the rebuilding of the Pallas Theater on Tuesday, November 4, 1879. But things weren't fairing well on the insurance side of the matter. Rumor was circulating that the insurance companies wanted to rebuild the theater instead of offering cash payment. McCormack and Sweeney filed suit, hiring Colonel Simeon Stansifer as their attorney. On Monday, November 10, the Royal Fire Association and the British American Insurance Companies announced they would contest the suits. Mr. H. Payton, attorney for the Royal Fire and British American Insurance companies, arrived in Columbus on Friday, November 14, for the purpose of working out a compromise.

By Friday, November 21, Colonel Stansifer announced that all parties in the matter of the Pallas Theater fire had settled. The Royal Fire Association and British American Insurance companies would pay McCormack and Sweeney $9,500, and McCormack and Sweeney would pay all other costs. With this matter at rest, no word was mentioned about rebuilding the theater. On Tuesday, November 25, 1879, the *Indianapolis Journal* had this to say: "Now, as a settlement between Messrs. Sweeney & McCormack and the insurance companies, these enterprising gentlemen will, in all probability, rebuild their business block; also the Theater."

However, the Columbus *Daily Evening Republican* of the same date offered forth this:

> *Yesterday morning, Mr. P.H. McCormack stated positively in Mr. J.I. Irwin's store that the firm would not build a theater, and he talked and counseled with Mr. Irwin upon the idea of the latter of transforming the old Christian Church into a theater. Later, a* Republican *reporter saw Mr. McCormack and spoke to him on the subject. He said he would not have a theater as a gift. This morning, our reporter again interviewed him on the subject, and the same time quoting the above article from the* Journal. *Mr. McCormack then said emphatically that the* Journal *correspondent was altogether wrong and added, "If say one was to build a theater on our walls and offer it to us as a gift, we would not accept it or have anything to do with it." This emphatic language settles the matter so far as McCormack & Sweeney are concerned.*

It is interesting to note that McCormack and Sweeney held as strong a conviction as Francis Crump had expressed regarding the rebuilding of his own opera house. At times, I have wondered if Francis might have rebuilt if his opera house had survived another four or five years. After all, Crump's hadn't even been open an entire year. A few more years, and a track record might have been established. But the Pallas *had* established a track record. It had been open for almost three and a half years. Yet McCormack and Sweeney elected not to rebuild and, as quoted, would not even accept one as a gift. I now believe that Francis would have been as emphatic after three years or even ten years. I also believe that the three capitalists lacked the knowledge needed in the day-to-day operations of running a theater or an opera house. This also includes the men they hired to act as managers. Their decisions also help to explain how difficult it was to make a profit from such a venture. Let's face it: no one was going to get rich from owning a theater. It was an extremely difficult way to earn a living in a town with less than five thousand people.

On Friday, December 19, McCormack and Sweeney received the last of their insurance payments on the Pallas Theater fire and could finally put the matter to rest. But were they now officially out of the amusement business?

January 1880 found people roller-skating inside Germania Hall when other amusements weren't happening. With Schwartzkopf's Germania being the only opera house remaining in Columbus, problems began to come forth. On Friday evening, March 12, Gus Phillips and his company came to town and performed the play *Under the Gas Light*. But the play didn't fare well. The stage was too small. The troupe could not use the necessary scenery, and excerpts from the play had to be cut to accommodate this lack of detail. On its departure, the troupe announced it would never return to Columbus.

This was a recurring complaint with Schwartzkopf's and the biggest drawback to his opera house ever setting the standard of a first-class place for amusements in Columbus. The more popular traveling shows of the day either heard through the grapevine that it lacked the necessary space that was required for their performances or outright refused to perform there due to its limited seating capacity. And to be honest, I cannot fault John Schwartzkopf in this matter. From the very beginning, his building was never designed to be an opera house. Initially, it fulfilled an immediate need. I believe he offered it as a place for amusements until someone else came forth and built an actual opera house. Alas, Schwartzkopf got stuck and did what he could with the place.

Although it had not been announced, a foretelling that the Pallas Theater would not be rebuilt occurred in March 1880. J.G. Schwartzkopf returned from Indianapolis with architectural drawings of a new stage layout for the Germania. Huber & Miller, architects, had based their drawings on the Indianapolis-based Park Theater stage. The new stage would be thirty feet deep and offer six wings with dressing rooms below. A railing would separate the orchestra pit from the audience, and theater boxes would be placed on either side of the stage area.

In April, word of a new theater began circulating around Columbus. It would be located in the rear of Davis's saloon on Third Street (this theater is believed to have been at the back of the Bissell Hotel property). The stage would be fifteen feet deep and fourteen feet wide—about half the size of the Germania. This variety theater was organized by Haney & Davis and Mr. Mears from Indianapolis was hired as manager. Henry Ranje, a local artist who had frescoed the south courtroom in the courthouse, painted the drop curtain. It was believed that everything would be ready for the grand opening on Tuesday, May 4. The theater was named the Third Street Variety Theater.

The Third Street Variety Theater did not offer the type of entertainment the cultural arts–seeking Columbus crowd was after. In the beginning, the shows were vulgar and rude. They catered to a citizen whose "refined taste" ran along the seedier, dirtier side. Nor was the auditorium anywhere close to the size of Schwartzopf's. It was much too small to ever be considered by national traveling shows of the day. Most shows were performed by local artists, with a few smaller troupes coming in from neighboring towns. But it wouldn't be around long. By August 1880, the Third Street Variety Theater was abandoned. The troupe involved changed its name to Theatre Comique and advertised that all shows would now be free of any and all vulgarities before hitting the road. Its first performance was at Schwartzkopf's Opera Hall on Friday, August 6, and after that, the troupe was never heard from (or about) again.

Meanwhile, although McCormack and Sweeney had been so emphatic about not rebuilding the Pallas Theater, the *Republican* continued to report updates on the progress of the opera house. On Tuesday, April 27, the gentlemen announced that applications were being received for a managerial position for the new opera house being built.

Had McCormack and Sweeney had a sudden change of heart? On Tuesday, May 11, 1880, as many as eleven merchants expressed an interest in renting the rooms underneath the new theater, and the following day, five large iron columns were received from Haugh & Company of Indianapolis for securing the theater floor. But work on the building was moving slow. McCormack and Sweeney were still undecided in their direction and what exactly would be offered on the second story. Six days later, the answer finally came. There would be no Pallas Theater. McCormack and Sweeney were now awaiting architectural drawings from Mr. Brown, Indianapolis architect. The site would offer a first-class forty-five-room hotel. The iron columns were taken out, and the upstairs floor was raised one foot. Plans for a three-story building were finally underway. The St. Denis Hotel would open on April 29, 1881.

The work on refitting Schwartzkopf's Opera Hall was completed in November 1880. A week before the opening of the opera season, new opera chairs were installed. The entrance had also been relocated to face Jackson Street. On Sunday evening, November 28, 1880, Schwartzkopf's Opera House reopened. Comedian John Thompson gave the opening performance in the new hall. While the *Evening Republican* praised the new additions of scenery, the drop curtain and improved acoustics, the reviewer was preoccupied with the new style of hats worn by patrons and the nuisance of not being able to fully appreciate watching the show (oh if he were only around today to witness cellphones!). The final touch to the opera house—carpeting—was added just before Christmas 1880.

1881

THE DEATH OF FRANCIS JEFFERSON CRUMP AND RUMORS OF NEW AMUSEMENT PLACES

The New Year of 1881 was rung in quietly on Columbus streets. A cold snap hit, with the temperature bottoming out at fourteen below zero. The Warner Comedy Company played Schwartzkopf's at the end of January and skipped town without paying boarding expenses at the Western House. Proprietor Stockdell followed the troupe to Shelbyville to get his money (and had to wait there for several days before he was paid). Then, on February 25, Howard Duffy, Joseph Condon, Joseph Irwin and Dr. W.O. Hogue, all leading citizens, met to arrange for the building of a new business block. Howard Duffy owned a parcel of land at the corner of Sixth and Washington Streets. The new building would offer businesses on the first floor and an opera hall on the second. In jest, the *Evening Republican* reported:

> *The new opera house building will be the eighth wonder of the world. It will have four store rooms on the ground floor, each reaching back to the alley and of commodious width. The ceiling of these will be of different heights, varying with the graduations of the floor of the hall, above which will rise from the pit to the gallery which will surround the dress circle and parquette. On each side of the large stage will be an immense telephone which will be connected with the telephone exchange we will have by the time the house is finished. The invalids and lazy people of the city will call up the exchange, ask to be connected with the opera house, and will then at their homes with a telephone to their ear hear every syllable spoken by the actors and the applause of the audience. Edison's latest invention for*

> *instantaneously photographing distant objects by electricity will also be put in by the management and rights sold. With one of these, the auditor in a distant part of the city will also be a spectator and after lying in bed and seeing and hearing a play will, at its conclusion, turn over and go to sleep while the audience is wading home through the snow and mud.*

While the paper undoubtedly had fun with such news, the parties concerned were serious about the opera hall. A cooper shop was removed in March, and plans were being made for construction.

The town of Columbus was entering a building boom. In addition to this new structure at Sixth and Washington, work was progressing very nicely on the St. Denis Hotel. Joseph Irwin would begin his new bank building at the northeast corner of Third and Washington. I.T. Brown, owner of the *Evening Republican* newspaper, purchased the parcel of land at the northeast corner of Fifth and Washington for the location of his new building. J.G. Schwartzkopf was intent on the erection of a new building at the southeast corner of Third and Washington.

In March 1881, Francis Crump hired architect L.L. Levering to draw up a sketch of a new building he planned on having erected. This Crump building would not be built at the corner of Fourth and Washington; it would be located on another parcel of F.J.'s prime downtown real estate holdings, situated across from the courthouse on the east side of Washington Street (just south of where Schwartzkopf would build). Levering's drawing of Crump's new building was put on display in the store window of Storey's bookstore.

Francis J. Crump would never see the finished product.

On Friday evening, April 29, 1881, a grand celebration was taking place at the southwest corner of Fifth and Washington Streets. Any thoughts of the old Pallas Theater were cast aside that evening, and the hoi polloi turned out in style to celebrate the opening of McCormack and Sweeney's St. Denis Hotel. People came from as far away as Jeffersonville, Louisville, Indianapolis and Cincinnati. Dinner for four hundred was served at midnight, and the party lasted until the 5:00 a.m. train bound for Louisville and Jeffersonville pulled out of the station. Around the time the 8:05 train carried the remaining partiers back home to Indianapolis, Francis J. Crump, now president of the First National Bank, was inside his private office, possibly trying to get caught up on a backlog of paperwork. He was still recovering from a severe illness that had kept him confined to his bed several weeks prior. He worked for a few hours before leaving for home about 11:00 a.m. Francis now lived in a house on the north end of Washington Street. His daughter, Elizabeth, and Elizabeth's husband, William J. Lucas, lived next door. Lucas worked with F.J. at the bank. On arriving home, Francis immediately took sick. Dr. Hudson was sent for. After Hudson left, Francis appeared to feel better, and by the afternoon, everything seemed fine. However, later that evening, Dr. Hudson stopped by to check on his condition and saw that his health was deteriorating rapidly. He sent William Lucas in search of the family.

At 10:30 p.m. on Saturday, April 30, 1881, Francis Jefferson Crump died at his home in the lone company of Dr. Hudson. The May 2 edition of the *Evening Republican* reported:

> *The effect of his death on the city and country will be great and not soon pass away. He was so directly and closely associated with a large part of the wealth of the county that the settlement of his estate will change many things. There are many acts of kindness which he did of which no one but his most intimate friends knew, and many a poor man unable to pay his rent has received a home for his family from the hands of his landlord. Thus ends the career of one of the most remarkable men Bartholomew County has ever produced. After 81 years of active existence, Francis J. Crump rests from his labors.*

The funeral was held at the home of Crump's son-in-law, William Lucas. Crump's body lay in a metallic casket weighing 575 pounds, his head resting on a bed of white flowers. Hundreds of people came to pay their respects. The casket was placed on a wagon by eight pallbearers, the place of interment being the old Crump Homestead, two miles north of the city. The procession following behind the funeral wagon was a mile in length.

At the time of his death, Francis J. Crump was one of seven millionaires in the state of Indiana. The twenty-year-old carpenter who had arrived in Bartholomew County with fifty cents in his pocket left in his wake a fortune. His estate was to be divided equally among his four living children, and in the days following his death, all money, stocks and bonds were disbursed. But Francis's vast real estate holdings would require some time. William Graves, Archie Teboe and James Godfrey were assigned to appraise all real estate holdings, including hundreds of acres in Columbus Township alone, thousands of acres of farmland in Bartholomew County and property holdings in Iowa and other states. An equitable division of his real estate holdings was finally disbursed in late 1881, with everything divided up between his four children: Francis T. (forty-four years old), Martha Crump Ruddick (forty-one years old), John S. (thirty-eight years old) and Elizabeth Crump Lucas (thirty-six years old).

Six weeks before Francis died, and one week after the announcement of his plans to rebuild the Crump building across from the courthouse, something very puzzling occurred. On March 16, 1881, Irwin, Duffy, Condon and Hogue announced they would not build an opera house on their property at Sixth and Washington. It is curious to note that another Columbus capitalist, who wished to remain anonymous and had large property holdings in the downtown area, intended to build a theater in the business district. The curious aspect of this is that leading up to and after the passing of Francis, not another word was mentioned regarding this new theater.

Could this anonymous person have been Francis Crump? It seems quite possible and even logical. There weren't many men who had large downtown property holdings, especially in the business part of town. Joseph Irwin can be ruled out. If he were that person, why didn't he follow through with the theater plans for the building at Sixth and Washington? J.G. Schwartzkopf can also be ruled out. In 1882, Schwartzkopf had the property at the southeast corner of Third and Washington rebuilt. If he was the anonymous person, why didn't his plans include a new theater in the construction? In addition to this, Schwartzkopf didn't own that much property in downtown Columbus. And that brings us back to Francis J. Crump. He most definitely fit the mysterious criteria. He owned more real estate in the business district of Columbus than any other capitalist. He was in the process of having a new building put up. So why not include a new theater in its design? Maybe he had a change of heart since the destruction of his opera hall seven years before. Maybe he was closer in touch with his own mortality and decided to leave an opera hall to the citizens of Columbus after his earthly departure. Alas, we shall never know for certain.

1881–88

JOHN SMITH CRUMP EMERGES

The Crump building that L.L. Levering had sketched out for Francis and displayed in the store window of Storey's bookstore was known as Commercial Row. This business district was situated on Washington Street, across from the new courthouse, and had been a downtown fixture since 1849.

The remodeling of Commercial Row began to take shape in October 1881. Mrs. J.B. Cobb owned the property directly south of Crump's and would be the first to remodel. Her building would be designed so the Crump building could adjoin hers, and possibly paying tribute to Francis, Mrs. Cobb elected to stay true to his design wishes.

The Crump portion of Commercial Row was inherited by Francis's youngest son, John. He was now the owner of the largest portion of the business block. On February 13, 1882, John met with a reporter from the *Evening Republican* newspaper to discuss his plans. He proclaimed, "This will not be a remodeled house at least so far as my portion is concerned, for the walls will be torn down, and a new building entire from the ground to the roof will be erected in its stead." John followed his father's direction and hired architect L.L. Levering to come up with a design for his new building that would also stay true to his father's original wishes. Once work was completed on his portion, J.G. Schwartzkopf would adjoin his new building on the north side of Crump's, and he would also hire Levering to design his portion.

This series of three buildings at that southeast corner of Third and Washington is what we see today. And it would be in this particular Crump building that John Crump would open his first theater in the town of Columbus, Indiana.

John Smith Crump came into this world in a bedroom on the Crump Homestead on February 24, 1843. He was Francis and Emilia's youngest son. At the time of John's birth, Francis and Emilia had already lost two children. Henry had died in 1839 at the age of twelve, while Sarah had died in 1832, just twenty-one days after her birth. To add to the list, seventeen days before John's third birthday, Emilia died. John would never know his mother.

John spent his first twelve years on the homestead, and in 1854, the family relocated to Columbus and into the house on Walnut (Fourth) Street. He attended both county and city schools. With the firing on of Fort Sumter on April 12, 1861, and twelve days shy of his eighteenth birthday, John abruptly quit school with the intent of joining the Union cause. His father had strictly forbid him to enlist, and with Columbus being such a small town, John knew there would be no possible way he could join up without his father finding out. John's solution was to run away, which he did, to Camp Noble in Madison, Indiana, where he enlisted in the Union army as a musician and became the youngest member of Company G, Twenty-second Regiment of the Indiana Volunteer Infantry. John Crump's time spent in the Union army was short, but it was long enough for the horrors of war to last him a lifetime. He was at the Battle of Pea Ridge, March 6–8, 1862, and by July was honorably discharged due to an unknown disability and sent home. He was quite ill when he got home, and his health continued to fail. Whatever sickness he had contracted has never been determined. Shortly after he returned home, the people of Columbus were thrown into a frenzied state by rumors that General John Hunt Morgan was making his way toward the town. A militia was formed, and the only way into the town on its western boundary was the Wagon Bridge at Second Street. The bridge was barricaded, and armed guards were posted. John's father, Francis, was one of the men who stood guard, as he had much to lose. Morgan, however, changed his course and went to Vernon instead.

On March 1, 1863, at the age of twenty, John Crump departed Columbus. Because of his health, doctors advised him to go west. He settled in Marysville, Kansas, with hopes that the western weather would improve his health. He opened a general store, met a young lady named Emma Webber and began courting her. On Sunday evening, April 9, 1865, the two were married. In reporting the news of the marriage, the April 13 edition of the *Marysville Kansas Enterprise* also added, "And

At eighteen, John Smith Crump was the youngest enlistee in Company G of the Twenty-second Regiment of Indiana Volunteers. *Courtesy of Randy Weinantz.*

you, Crump, we hate to part with you, but Fate has scattered our entreaties to the winds. We have known you just long enough to admire your genial disposition, and your every action has been proof that you possess the qualities which constitute an honorable gentleman. Our most kind wishes go with you as you journey through the long years on the happy road of married life."

John Crump and his new wife moved back to Columbus, but they (most likely his wife) did not like living here and in 1866 relocated once again to Kansas. The couple spent a short time in Marysville and then uprooted and moved to Manhattan, Kansas, with John opening a general store. Finally, in 1869, they made their final move back to Columbus. Upon moving back, John and Emma took up residence at the old Crump Homestead. Between 1883 and 1887, John had a two-story Italianate house built at the northwest corner of Seventh and Mechanic (Lafayette) Streets. The family would share its residency between this house and the Crump Homestead.

John Crump opened his first theater sometime between 1882 and 1888 on the second story of his building on Washington Street in the new Commercial Row. While there is definite proof he had a theater at this location, and prior to his theater on Third Street, there is no definitive proof that much of anything ever occurred there! In searching through copies of the *Evening Republican* from 1882 through 1888, there were no weekly advertisements for upcoming attractions ever published. There were no reviews of any troupes ever performing at this Washington Street theater. The only solid proof shows up in the December 23, 1888 edition of the paper, where on the last page, a three-inch block-style advertisement announced that on January 1, 1889, J.S. Crump's theater would have a "Grand New Year's Performance." The Misses Deaves would appear on stage with comedians Harry Mack and Harry Potter for a performance of the musical comedy *Chaos Flat.*

Photo of John Crump (left) and an unidentified man, possibly taken in Marysville, Kansas. *Courtesy of Randy Weinantz.*

The southeast corner of Third and Washington (Commercial Row) and John Crump's first theater. *Courtesy of the* Republic.

There are far too many unanswered questions regarding John Crump's first theater to offer anything more than speculation. It would be easy for me to fill up an entire chapter with speculative ideas, and I have neither the time nor the luxury for such in this book. So at this point in time, I will state this much and move on: this first theater was not to his liking, nor did the building offer what was required to fulfill his desires of providing a first-class opera palace to the citizens of Columbus. It was simply lacking in too many details.

PART 2

THE CRUMP THEATRE

1889
THE BUILDING OF CRUMP'S NEW THEATRE

Colonel John A. Keith was Columbus, Indiana's own Civil War hero. Before the war, he studied law with Hubbard and Sexton in Rushville, Indiana, and around 1855 moved to Columbus and set up his law firm. He married Melissa Crisler on November 1, 1859. A daughter, May Dema, was born to the couple in January 1861. Six weeks after his daughter's birth, Keith's wife died. When Fort Sumter was attacked, Keith helped form the Twenty-first Indiana. He was seriously wounded at a battle in Baton Rouge on August 5, 1862, and would never fully recover. He remained in service, though, and was promoted to colonel on March 22, 1863. With the end of the war, he returned to Columbus to practice law.

In 1871, Colonel Keith had Keith's Arcade built. This beautiful two-story building was situated on the south side of Tipton (Third Street) in the middle of the block between Washington and Franklin Streets. It was called an arcade because of the many arches that graced the front of the building. It was in this building that Keith had his law office, and between 1871 and 1889, Keith's Arcade was home to a number of different merchants and businesses. The *Republican* newspaper began operations in the building in 1872, and at one time or another, the rooms inside Keith's Arcade were filled with doctor's offices, grocery outlets, restaurants, a clothing store and a plumbing supply store. In 1874, Snipes and Adams opened their dining hall on the first floor and also took in day boarders. But the one thing Keith's Arcade was not was a place where amusements were held.

After the war, Colonel Keith was not a well man. He made numerous trips to West Baden, Indiana, to take advantage of the healing powers of the sulphur springs there. His sojourns to West Baden would sometimes last as long as a month. He was known to drink heavily, possibly his way of trying to find a little comfort from his war wounds. He was committed to the insane asylum in Indianapolis on more than one occasion, and on the morning of December 3, 1888, Sheriff William Smith took him back to the asylum to be recommitted.

At the time he was committed, Colonel Keith owed Francis T. Crump (Frank), John's elder brother, $28,000. On January 24, 1889, a guardian's sale of real estate was announced in the *Evening Republican*. David Stobo had been assigned as Colonel Keith's guardian, and most if not all of Keith's property holdings were to be sold at auction. The auction took place in the north room of the courthouse on January 28, 1889. There was a good turnout, and the lots brought in a good deal more than what was anticipated. After Frank Crump's claim of $28,000 was discharged, a gross profit of over $6,000 was realized.

John Crump was one of the bidders in the north room that morning. His wishes were to purchase Lot 14, a prime piece of real estate located in the heart of downtown Columbus. Bidding on this property brought in more money than any other lot sold that day, and as the final call was shouted, John's bid stood at $6,000. He was now the new owner of Lot 14, better known as the Keith Arcade property.

Immediately, John commenced with preparations of turning the arcade building into a first-class theater. This new theater would, at last, fulfill the needs and wants of both the community and traveling shows of the day. Its physical size would be large enough to seat more than twice the number of people as Schwartzkopf's Opera House, but more importantly, the stage would be large enough to meet the requirements and demands of more prominent, national troupes of the day. Many of these troupes traveled with their own scenery, and due to the limitations at Schwartzkopf's Opera House, they could not set up the necessary backdrops. When Sid C. Frances and company performed the play *Jealousy* at Schwartzkopf's in December 1888, only one-third of their scenery could be used. This had a negative impact on the audience as well as the performers, and because of these types of issues, it was not uncommon for acting companies to refuse a return engagement.

John Crump was more than aware of these problems, and he paid particular attention to address such issues during the planning stages of his theater. He had much experience to draw on, what with the faults of Schwartzkopf's, as well as his own father's opera house. He did not rush anything, instead taking his time to meticulously think over every small detail. This was it. This was his chance. While the term "opera house" had been loosely used to describe each prior attempt (Keith's Hall, his father's opera house, Schwartzkopf's and the Pallas Theater), John's intent and desire was to offer the town of Columbus its first true, stand-alone opera house—one that would satisfy both the theatergoing crowd and the acting companies. He wanted to give the people of Columbus the best money could buy.

In February 1889, John befriended William Riley. Riley was the manager of Riley's Dramatic Company, which had performed in Columbus dating back as far as John's father's opera house. Riley had spent his entire lifetime in the theater. His input was invaluable. He shared with John what was necessary from an acting company's viewpoint, and together they addressed such topics as the location and layout of dressing rooms, the need for warmth and comfort of such and the layout of the stage and auditorium.

Keith's Arcade was noted for the beautiful arches on its façade. *Drawing by Lesley Carter.*

John hired architect Charles Sparrell to design his new theater. He was particularly fascinated with the Grand Opera House in Madison, Indiana, and on March 1, 1889, arranged with Sparrell and Riley to travel to that city to inspect it. At the last minute, Riley had to bow out. John, accompanied by his wife, his daughter and Charles Sparrell, traveled to Madison on March 8. John liked what he saw. His new theater would be patterned on the theater in Madison. Returning to Columbus, Sparrell began working on plans for Crump's new theater. Its location would indeed be at the Keith Arcade site. On March 19, John met with jeweler Fred Donner and bought from him the adjoining property required for his new theater.

Crump's new theater now had a name: the New Arcade Theatre.

Charles Sparrell completed his drawings and specifications on the theater the first week of April. Buildings on the east and south side of the arcade were already in the process of being removed, and on April 9, contractors were notified, and the process of working up bids began. On April 22, bids for the construction of the theater were opened. Five contractors had submitted bids: Dunlap and Coats ($15,196), Keller and Brockman ($14,975), Glanton and Cotton ($15,748), Hege and Company ($15,400) and Joseph C. Condon ($15,500). Keller and Brockman were awarded the contract.

Charles Sparrell was a busy man in early 1889. Not only had the Columbus architect prepared drawings and specifications for John Crump's New Arcade Theatre, but in a period from March 26 to April 13, he drew up plans and specifications for H. Griffith and Eli Marquette's new elevator at Third and Lafayette Streets, Dr. Falk's new residence on Washington Street, Dr. Mennet's home in Jonesville, Mrs. Emma Bruvoork's residence on Pearl Street, a new storeroom in Elizabethtown, a residence in Edinburg and a new Lutheran church in Seymour. Regarding Crump's new theater, he shared the following comment, which appeared in the April 15, 1889 edition of the *Evening Republican*: "Few people have any idea of the amount of work it takes to prepare the plans of a building the size of the New Arcade opera house. An estimate has to be made of the weight of every particle of material which is put in the building in order to know what strength to make the structure."

Amid all this work, Sparrell also found time to contact several Chicago companies that specialized in first-class opera house scenery and furniture, requesting estimates from each. Representatives from several Chicago firms came to Columbus to show samples of their merchandise. In addition to this request, John Crump contacted several nationally recognized scenic artists at that time for the purpose of submitting bids on the scenic requirements for the theater. By May 18, work on the construction of the New Arcade Theatre was progressing quite nicely. The weather was cooperating in the effort. The foundation was finished, and work commenced on the construction of the exterior brick walls.

John was more than pleased with both the work and the planning that had gone into his theater's construction. On May 18, 1889, he told a reporter with the *Evening Republican* that the building would be better than he had initially contemplated and that it was his intention to make it about ten years ahead of the city in the matter of it being a strictly first-class theater. John had now hired his son-in-law, Richard Gottschalk, as manager of the theater. Gottschalk was already busying himself with issuing circulars to the managers of top-rated performing arts companies across the country announcing the fall opening of the new theater.

By June, a Chicago scenic company had been chosen to provide the interior work. Perry Landis, with Sosman and Landis, was in Columbus to meet with John and go over ideas for the drop curtain. It was decided that scenes of Sicily would be used for the drop curtain and that the artist responsible would be Thomas G. Moses, a nationally recognized artist of the day. Work was also now underway on the stage scenery. Many different scenes would need to be painted to reflect the mood of various elements of a play, as well as standard backdrops for particular rooms of a home, castle or dungeon. In addition to the actual sceneries, the mechanics of moving them were also incorporated as part of the job.

Construction of the New Arcade Theatre moved smoothly, quickly and efficiently throughout the summer months. The actual theater building itself was a new addition, adjoining the old Keith Arcade building at its south side. During the construction of the theater portion, there was also a remodel of the old Keith Arcade portion. The original Keith Arcade building was separated into three distinct sections. The three arches at the top housed, underneath each arch, a separate building within the main building. The layout would remain this way. The left and right portions of the building would be rented out to businesses, and the middle section would become the entranceway into the theater. The first merchant to rent space from John Crump was Frank Pancake. His place of business was on the right side of the entranceway, or on the west side of the building. In early August, he began remodeling his part with the purpose of offering up a first-class saloon.

A few days after Frank Pancake started work on his saloon, Keller and Brockman were wrapping up their work. The weather and the number of workers they employed both cooperated beyond their wildest expectations. They finished the job three weeks early. The major emphasis now turned to decorating the interior.

As the completion of the New Arcade Theatre was now only weeks away, George Schwartzkopf decided to spruce up his opera house, too. He hired Charlie Fowler to paint and repaper the interior and touch up the scenery. He also replaced the seats with more comfortable and plush opera chairs.

On Thursday evening, September 12, 1889, Frank Pancake opened his elegant new saloon in Crump's theater building. If this would be any indication of the caliber of class that could be anticipated of the theater itself, the citizens of Columbus were in for a treat. Pancake's saloon was the finest, most luxurious saloon in all of Columbus. Hundreds of people turned out for the opening. Pancake secured the services of the City Band to perform out front.

The opening of Crump's New Theatre was less than seven weeks away.

With work progressing nicely inside the auditorium, Crump Theatre manager Richard Gottschalk was intent on providing a cosmopolitan choice for opening night. In early September, he turned his attention to securing a particular opera company from Chicago and an opera by Charles Lecocq. In 1879, Lecocq composed the opera *The Pretty Persian*, and the Norcross Opera Company, a newly formed Chicago-based troupe, was performing it in its hometown. Through much effort and determination on the part of Gottschalk, the Norcross Opera Company eventually committed to appear on opening night. The cost to get them to Columbus was exorbitant, and Gottschalk assured the troupe that a good crowd would be on hand and that the citizens of Columbus would be very appreciative of their performance. After weeks of negotiation, the Norcross Opera Company finally committed to the October engagement on September 17.

The October 5, 1889 edition of the *Evening Republican* offered up a rather lengthy article with the caption, "John S. Crump as Benefactor of Columbus." The article provided a brief history of the American theater scene, from its inception after the Revolutionary War to what was then the present day. After the history lesson, the paper offered the following:

> *For many years, Columbus waited for its enrollment in the category of theatrical cities. Its people enjoyed the benefits of the march of progress in every other way, but it is only after long and patient waiting and after the failure of several praiseworthy ventures that we, at this late hour,*

> *are enabled to gratify our wish to cultivate and show our appreciation of dramatic art. Should the people of this city, therefore, not be truly grateful to Mr. John S. Crump, who, recognizing this universal want of our city, shows a public spiritedness and liberality toward his fellow citizens such as has never been equaled in Columbus, in that he has erected a theater second to none in any city several times the size of Columbus, in the United States, and thus opened up a new avenue to the amusement loving public, where they may see and study dramatic art as presented on a stage equal in every respect to those of the great metropolitan theaters.*

John Smith Crump, benefactor, was on the verge of accomplishing something that may have seemed almost impossible to some in a town of roughly five thousand people. As with the magnificent courthouse of McCormack and Sweeney in 1874, Crump's New Theatre would stand as a monument to what man could accomplish. A new degree of sophistication and cultivation was about to make its debut performance in the town of Columbus, Indiana.

It is not known when Crump's Theatre Orchestra was formed. The orchestra had been performing at local events since May 1889. On October 7, the orchestra performed at the opening of the White House, a dry goods store on Washington Street. Mr. A. Weslow had opened his dry goods business in 1867. His business was so great that, in 1889, he had a building addition added on. To celebrate the reopening, and also to promote the opening of Crump's New Theatre, the band entertained the masses. A half-page newspaper ad was bought and advertised, among other things, ladies' opera wraps. Crump's Theatre Orchestra also performed on October 10 at the opening of the Post Office Saloon.

Also unknown is exactly when the name of the theater changed. What was originally the "New Arcade Theatre" somehow got changed as the months progressed. By October, it became known as "Crump's New Theatre." During the remodel of the Keith Arcade façade, the words "Keith's Arcade A.D. 1871" were removed within the three arches at the top of the building. In their place, inlaid brickwork now spelled out the words "Crump's New Theatre."

The final touches to the theater were taking place. Carpeting was put down on October 12, and the decorative work inside the theater was close to completion. Tuesday, October 15 saw the opening of W.C. Heaton's restaurant. His business was located on the left side of the entranceway, or the east side of the building. As with Frank Pancake, Heaton rented the upstairs portion of his side, too. In addition to the restaurant, he offered two rooms to be used as either apartments or for day boarders.

Many men had made this moment in Columbus happen. The brick masons, carpenters, plumbers, gas fitters and painters that took part in the construction will never be known. A few of the people who have been recognized include Keller and Brockman, a local contracting firm; Mr. F.A. Brown of Maxwell and Company (Chicago), who furnished the supplies for the interior decoration; Charles Gilbert, T.B. Benhan, George Beckman and Charles Green, who did the frescoing and painting of the inside; Henry Strassner, finish carpenter; and Sosman and Landis, who hand painted the beautifully crafted sceneries.

Possibly as a final farewell to John Crump's first theater on Washington Street, a celebration ball was held on Thursday evening, October 17, 1889.

The grand opening of Crump's New Theatre was less than two weeks away.

The town of Columbus had come a long way since Keith's Hall was the town's so-called opera house. Keith's Hall, Francis J. Crump's Opera House, Schwartzkopf's and the Pallas Theater had all been noble attempts at establishing the cultivation and sophistication "final piece of the pie" that had been missing in the town's overall development. The pioneering fathers who had tried to bring this cultural and sophisticated piece into the equation, in all actuality, did not have the knowledge and foresight to accomplish this objective. That fact alone sets John Crump apart from the men who had tried earlier. It had taken seventeen years for just the right man to come along. And John Crump was the right man. His knowledge, experience and foresight reflected his true determination to succeed where others had failed. John Crump was indeed a visionary. To dedicate so much time and effort to this project was something his predecessors possibly did not have the luxury of doing. After all, Schwartzkopf was a wagon builder. McCormack and Sweeney were contractors. Francis J. Crump was an investor. And to me, this explains a lot. While each of them was outstanding in their own fields, it would take a different mindset to give Columbus a top-notch place for the dramatic arts. The men that had preceded John Crump had all shaped the town through their hard work. They gave people jobs. Their tax dollars provided schools. Before today's welfare system, they helped take care of the poor. Their efforts and strengths had made Columbus a nice place to raise a family and to call home. Columbus was a prosperous, growing community made up of men who cared. It had the best to offer in the way of jobs, schools, churches and fraternal organizations. And through the establishment of a first-class theater, John Crump put the final touches on the canvas, making the city of Columbus complete.

1889

THE OPENING OF CRUMP'S NEW THEATRE

On October 29, 1889, the day before opening night, the *Evening Republican* offered up a detailed walkthrough of what the public could expect:

> *Passing through the massive archway that forms the main entrance to the theater, the visitor finds himself in a spacious and well-lighted vestibule, the ceiling and walls of which are decorated in dull tones and gold relief work, treated in strict harmony with the decorations in general, and is of the Romanesque style. To the right and left rise, the commodious staircases lead to the balcony, under which, in the lobby, is located an inglenook. The box office, with large sliding window, and an art window to either side, is located on the right side. At the end of the lobby, the entrance to the auditorium is reached, and the charming and graceful order of architecture and decoration, which prevails throughout the auditorium, asserts itself at once. The designs for the entire decorative work are composite productions from modern temples of dramatic art. The carpet for the boxes, parquet and aisles were furnished by L. Lehman and are in perfect keeping with the remainder of the decorations. The chairs in the lower part of the house are a rich red plush back, with perforated mahogany seats, and in the remainder of the house, of perforated cherry, back and seats, all on the latest improved automatic iron frames. The balcony projects over the orchestra circle, the ceiling of which is like that of a room elegantly decorated with graceful design in pink and gold. The massive proscenium arch of thirty feet opening is richly ornamented with relief work siennas and gold. The rails of the*

proscenium boxes, fashion boxes and balcony are of red plush, and their rich color constitutes a pleasing relief to the delicate tints that prevail throughout the auditorium. From the top of the immense proscenium arch rises the ceiling by a succession of graceful coves extending across the house, following the line of vision to the back seats of the gallery. The entire ceiling is divided into panels, separated by ornamental bands of plastic relief. The decoration of the ceiling, like that of the entire house, is outlined in gold relief. Perhaps the handsomest feature of the auditorium are the angular pagodas that form the proscenium boxes and stand out in graceful symmetry, giving an uninterrupted view of the stage and adding greatly to the elegance of the interior. The proscenium boxes, of which there are two on either side, one above the other, are elaborately ornamented and hung with draperies of rich silk colorings, with flowing fringes and heavy brocatelle portieres. To the right and left, adjoining the proscenium boxes, are four elegantly fitted fashion boxes, two on each side. The balcony has five rows of automatic folding chairs, back of which large and commodious settees ascent at an angle in the line of vision to the top of the gallery, offering an unobstructed view of the stage from any position. The balcony is provided with two large exits by broad stairways, leading into the spacious lobby below. All the exits leading from the auditorium are furnished with paneled doors opening outward, either directly to the level of the street, or to spacious stairways. With the abundant precautions taken in the way of reels of hose hung in available spaces, the absence of combustible material and the great number of exits, nothing but an absolute panic can prevent the audience from leaving the house with perfect safety and comfort in two minutes. Every door in the vast auditorium is an exit.

Absolute harmony in every detail of ornamentation and coloring pervades the interior of the building, and the decorations, executed by Messrs. Charles Green, George Beckman, T.B. Denham, and Charles Gilbert, are artistically beautiful and correct in design, the charming scheme of color extending to the rich curtain, which is in perfect harmony with the decorations. The stage of Crump's theater is in perfect keeping with the magnificent auditorium and is furnished with every available device and improvement necessary to insure realistic presentations. Messrs. Sosman and Landis, the celebrated scenic artists of Chicago, have furnished a large and most comprehensive stock of scenery which can be made into over 30 complete and beautiful stage pictures. The drop curtain represents a scene in Palermo, a beautiful and appropriate picture of life in Sicily, which also is in complete harmony with decorations of the theater and was painted

> *by the eminent artist Thomas G. Moses. The handling of the color, with the brilliant effect of a southern sun, a clear blue sky and the rich coloring of the dresses of the wanderers and the lazy native, presents a charming picture which is beautifully framed by an artistic arrangement of heavy silk and plush drapery of rich though somber colors. The steps and floor on which the pictures rest are partly covered with heavy oriental rugs, the tormentors and draperies are in plush and silk, and for concert and lecture purposes, there is a modern fancy chamber in the prevailing composite decoration, with pale blue and gold walls, and an antique oak interior in the Romanesque order of architecture. The working sets comprise a full line of palace drops, a Norman armor gothic with brilliant light effects. French interior of Louis XIV, Roman interior, rustic kitchen, prison, plain interior, garret with ceiling and skylight, dark wood scenes, ancient street, modern street, cottage flats, snow landscape, village landscape, moonlight castle, light wood landscape, mountain pass, ocean scene and horizon, set houses and cottages, and a very large list of battlements and garden walls, wharf pieces, village sets, trees, balustrades, vases, tents, cottages, huts, bridges, etc. The stage measures 30 feet by 60 feet by 42 feet. The stage machinery has been put in under the supervision of Mr. C.S. King of Chicago, in which he was assisted by Mr. Walter Doup, who is a stage machinist with a thorough knowledge of the business, and who will have charge of this department of the theater. There are Hamlet, star and vampire traps, and every contrivance that is known to modern stage mechanism. Altogether, the scenic investiture of the stage of Crump's Theater will not be surpassed by that of any other stage in the country.*

It had taken more than seventeen years for the first, true opera house/theater to make its debut in the small town of Columbus, Indiana. The curtain was about to go up.

Not since the erection of the courthouse by McCormack and Sweeney in 1874 had the *Evening Republican* newspaper kept its readers abreast of the events unfolding on any other building in such great detail. John Crump may have spent his own money in the construction, but in a much grander sense, his was a theater for the people. The paper proclaimed:

> *The magnificent building will stand as a monument of the public spirit of Mr. John S. Crump, for it cannot be looked upon as a private speculation, as the same money invested in other enterprises would have earned much better returns. The erection of the theater is the response to a constant demand,*

A circa 1897 photograph of Walter Doup and an unidentified young man taken in front of Crump's Theatre. *Courtesy of Carol Ahlbrand.*

Quite possibly the earliest glimpse of Crump's New Theatre interior (circa 1890s). *Courtesy of Randy Weinantz.*

> *stretching back over a number of years, made by the press and public for better accommodations for enjoying legitimate amusement. In response to this demand, Mr. Crump concluded to open up a new avenue to the theater-going public second to none in any city of the size of Columbus in America.*

Crump's New Theatre brought along with its opening a sense of civic pride truly not felt since the dedication of the courthouse. Trying to wrap one's mind around this importance in today's world probably seems so foreign and unusual to us all, but to the citizens of an 1889 Columbus, it meant the world. The time had finally arrived for first-class presentations in the field of dramatic arts. The theatergoing crowd could enjoy the same high-class amusements as other, much larger cities across the country. There would be no further concerns with a stage being too small, and Crump's New Theatre could accommodate more than twice the number of people as Schwartzkopf's Opera House.

The evening of October 30, 1889, was a stormy one. A gully washer erupted just as people began filling up Crump's New Theatre. Once inside, the theatergoing crowd was treated to the sweet sounds of Wil Schnur and the Crump's Theatre Orchestra. Possibly the highlight of the evening was the performance of Fred Frear. Frear had an extensive history in the field of amusements. He had played with the Stewart Opera Company in St. Louis and the Comley-Barton and McCaul Companies in New York and, at one time, toured the country with his own company. From St. Louis to Boston to New York to small-town Columbus, Indiana, his excellence would become typical of the kind of amusements the city of Columbus would come to expect. Both Frear and Miss Mae Worden were so popular during the evening's opening engagement that they were called back three times by an enthusiastic audience. It is highly doubtful that anyone attending the performance walked away unsatisfied.

The finality of the evening—the cheers from the crowded auditorium, the appreciation of the work that had gone into the creation of a theater so beautiful—must have been somewhat overwhelming to John Crump. It had come at no small expense. He had given the citizens of Columbus the best that money could buy. Take Mr. C.S. King, for example. King was a stage machinist and carpenter employed by Chicago-based firm Sosman and Landis. King began working in the field in 1859 and had applied his talents in the construction of some of the finest opera houses in the United States, Canada and Mexico. His knowledge in the field was unsurpassed, and John Crump deferred to him a trust based on

Crump's New Theatre, circa 1893. *Courtesy of Tamara Stone Iorio.*

his knowledge. The scenery mechanisms he built worked perfectly on opening night. It ran so perfect and smooth that no one noticed.

October 30, 1889, was the beginning of a new era in Columbus, Indiana entertainment. John Crump had succeeded beyond anyone's expectations. He had opened the door to a higher culture not witnessed by the city before. His public spiritedness put on display that evening would not be his final curtain call.

1890–99

J.S. CRUMP'S RAILWAY, THE BELVEDERE HOTEL AND JOHN CRUMP'S TESTIMONIAL

According to the 1890 Sanborn Insurance Map, the population of Columbus was eight thousand people. The town now spread itself out as far north as Sixteenth Street. The American Starch Works, a massive, sprawling business enterprise, was located at the northwest boundary of the town at Sixteenth and Washington Streets. It was mammoth in size, consisting of one huge U-shaped building, a warehouse, gluten cisterns, a massive corncrib, a feeding house, hog pens and a separate office building. Joseph Irwin paid George Dahn $8,125 for sixteen acres of land, the property lines including everything north of Fifth Street to the east–west alley north of Sixth Street and extending east to the Haw Creek. The development of the Maple Grove addition would commence in a few months. On May 9, 1890, a select group of men from Crawfordsville, Indiana, paid a visit to the fair city of Columbus. The mayor, mayor-elect and city officers numbered fourteen in all and were received at Crump's Theatre by Columbus's mayor and a group of esteemed citizens, including John Crump and Crump Theatre manager Richard Gottschalk. That evening, all attended Crump's Theatre to watch Fred Bock and his New York cast appear in *Streets of New York*. To close out the month, on May 29, 1890, a special meeting of the city council was called. The franchise for a streetcar system was received, entered and approved.

John Crump was about to give the city of Columbus its first mass transit system. Estimated cost of the project was $16,000.

Crump's Street Railway would make a loop, with the track beginning at Third and Washington Streets, going north on Washington to Eleventh and turn east to Pearl Street, then north to Sixteenth Street, east to Chestnut, south to Eleventh, west to Sycamore and south to Third Street before finally connecting at the corner of Third and Washington. Once the line was completed, it would cover a distance of three miles. The city ordinance allowed 120 days for Crump to complete it.

Work began immediately, as time was of the essence. The railway was to be completed by October 1. One thing that would rule in John Crump's favor was the care that the city of Columbus paid to the condition of its streets, all of which had been graded and were already fairly level. This would be one less item to consider.

By July 20, 1890, ties for Crump's Street Railway had been laid as far as Sycamore Street. More than fifty men were employed by Crump and were making noted progress. The rails were being poured by a company outside of Columbus and were expected to ship the following week. In early August, John Crump was informed that the five street cars he ordered from a firm in St. Louis were ready for service and had an estimated date of delivery of August 18. Shortly around this time, all ties in the route had been laid. With the ties secured, the contracting firm of Scott and Lyle spent the remaining five weeks laying rails for Crump's railway. They provided both the product and labor, completing the job by September 9.

Crump's streetcar line opened to the public on September 15, 1890, fifteen days ahead of schedule. The mule-powered trolley cars made the initial route with Columbus's most prominent citizens in the first car. The public was invited to enjoy an hour's worth of free rides following. Crump's Street Railway was laid out to incorporate every part of the city. The venture was a progressive move for a city of eight thousand. Columbus residents could boast not only of having one of the finest courthouses in the state of Indiana but also one of the finest theaters in southern Indiana and, now, its first mass transit system.

Within a period of one year, John Crump had given both a first-class theater and the city's first mass transit system to the citizens of Columbus. Does a picture begin to form in your mind as to the kind of person John Crump was? What shaped the man? What important chapters of his life had determined these events? Had the fact of never knowing his mother played a part? Did the horrors of war have a profound effect? Had his time spent on the westernmost boundary of civilization opened his eyes to

Crump's New Theatre and Crump's railway, circa 1893. *Courtesy of Randy Weinantz.*

a greater purpose? I believe it was a combination of all those things, but only speculation can be drawn from his actions. Surely, the money and property he inherited could have been used for more profitable business ventures than a theater and a railway. But the picture beginning to shape at this point clearly depicts a man whose purpose in life stretched far beyond the almighty dollar.

Crump's Street Railway provided local residents a convenient means by which any part of the city could be reached, whether it was getting to and from work, shopping or visiting someone on the other side of town. It also provided a comfortable way to travel to his theater.

There was one final piece to put in place.

On the evening of September 29, 1890, Robert Downing appeared on stage at Crump's Theatre. Downing performed the stage play *The Gladiator*, accompanied by Miss Eugenie Blair. Blair would become Downing's second wife. The marriage would not last, as he would marry a third time, to Miss Helene Kirkpatrick. Miss Kirkpatrick had appeared at both Schwartzkopf's and F.J. Crump's opera house on several occasions.

It would be a dauntless task to compile a list of all performances at Crump's Theatre. Suffice it to say at this point in time that many well-renowned acts and an equal number of terrible ones performed at Crump's. These acts, the traveling cast members, all needed accommodations during their stay. Some preferred to travel with their own scenery, which was delivered to Crump's Theatre on arrival. The majority of the prodigious troupes of the day required first-class accommodations and were put up at the St. Denis Hotel. The Bissell Hotel, located across the street from Crump's Theatre and at the corner of Third and Franklin, had seen better days. It had changed hands several times since its opening in 1875 and was no longer the shining jewel of Columbus lodging. That status would now fall to the St. Denis. But the St. Denis was two and a half blocks away from the theater. It is possible that some troupes put up at the Western Hotel at the southwest corner of Second and Jackson Streets. Although it was closer to the theater, it was hardly the type of place in which a theater manager would want members of a nationally prominent troupe to stay. John Crump came up with an answer to logistics: he bought the Bissell Hotel.

In the 1860s, the Bissell was called the McEwen Block. Before east–west street names were changed in the summer of 1879, the McEwen Block was situated at the northwest corner of Tipton (Third) and Franklin Streets. It was named after William McEwen, another city pioneer and another rags-to-riches story—only in McEwen's case, it was back to rags again. McEwen had played a role in Columbus's first bank, B.F. Jones and Company. In 1865, the bank became McEwen and Sons, but by 1871, it suffered a catastrophic failure. City funds on deposit to the tune of almost $100,000 were wiped out. It would take twelve years for the courts to resolve the matter, the case reaching as high as the Indiana State Supreme Court. The McEwen Block was

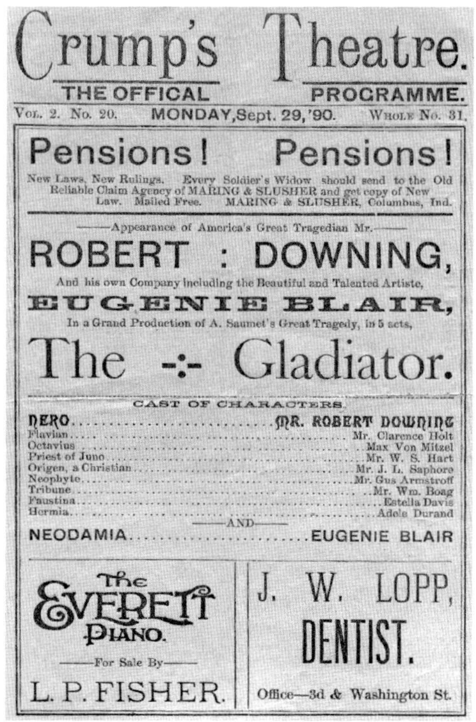

Crump's Theatre.
THE OFFICAL PROGRAMME.
VOL. 2. NO. 20. MONDAY, Sept. 29, '90. WHOLE NO. 31.

Pensions! Pensions!
New Laws, New Rulings. Every Soldier's Widow should send to the Old Reliable Claim Agency of MARING & SLUSHER and get copy of New Law. Mailed Free. MARING & SLUSHER, Columbus, Ind.

—Appearance of America's Great Tragedian Mr.—
ROBERT : DOWNING,
And his own Company including the Beautiful and Talented Artiste,
EUGENIE BLAIR,
In a Grand Production of A. Saumet's Great Tragedy, in 5 acts,
The -:- Gladiator.

CAST OF CHARACTERS.

NERO.......MR. ROBERT DOWNING
Flavian.......Mr. Clarence Holt
Octavius.......Max Von Mitzel
Priest of Juno.......Mr. W. S. Hart
Origen, a Christian.......Mr. J. L. Saphore
Neophyte.......Mr. Gus Armstroff
Tribune.......Mr. Wm. Boag
Faustina.......Estella Davis
Hermia.......Adele Durand
—AND—
NEODAMIA.......EUGENIE BLAIR

The EVERETT PIANO.
—For Sale By—
L. P. FISHER.

J. W. LOPP,
DENTIST.
Office—3d & Washington St.

An 1890 Crump Theatre program for Robert Downing's *Gladiator* performance. *Courtesy of Randy Weinantz.*

purchased by George Bissell in 1875, becoming his Bissell Hotel the same year. John Crump bought the Bissell property in early 1891 for the purpose of providing a first-class hotel a mere stone's throw from his theater. He would name his hotel the Belvedere.

John Crump's Belvedere Hotel was the largest and most modern hotel in southern Indiana. It included a bar, a billiard room, a reading room and multiple lavatories on each floor. On the evening of December 1, 1891, a grand ball was given by John Crump in celebration of the opening. More than 200 people were present for the festivities. Professor Mason's orchestra provided the music, with Mr. James McKeehan of Indianapolis fulfilling the role of dancing director. Dinner was served for 160 at midnight, with dancing continuing until the wee hours of the morning.

The west end of the Belvedere Hotel was situated directly across the street from Crump's Theatre. Its location was perfect for traveling shows of the day. But John Crump had added something unique to both buildings during construction: he had a tunnel dug underneath Third Street connecting the hotel to his theater. Actors and actresses of the day could make their way through the tunnel and enter the theater underneath the stage. There would no longer be a need to walk across muddy old Third Street!

Before I put this matter to bed, there is another unique historical feature regarding the Belvedere Hotel that should be mentioned. That McEwen Block property dated back to 1863. At that time, a select group of Columbus capitalists—C.B. Kerr, A. Pine and Dr. J.F. Wright—were in the foundry business, the group assuming the name Kerr, Pine and Company. At the time the runner-type rails of the JM&I Railroad were being replaced with the newer "I" rail design, the foundry bought up a large quantity of the cast-iron shoes that held the original iron runners onto planks of wood. When the original McEwen block was built, there was an exterior iron stairway leading up to the second story. At the request of McEwen, the foundry took the cast-iron shoes, recycled the product and provided steps for the stairway. During construction of the Belvedere, this stairway was remodeled. By order of John Crump, three of the old steps were saved and became the first three steps on the interior staircase inside the hotel. I wonder if those old stair pieces were still around when the Belvedere Hotel was destroyed by fire in February 1967. I wonder if anyone around at that time was aware of the historical significance of those steps and the tie to our city's first railroad.

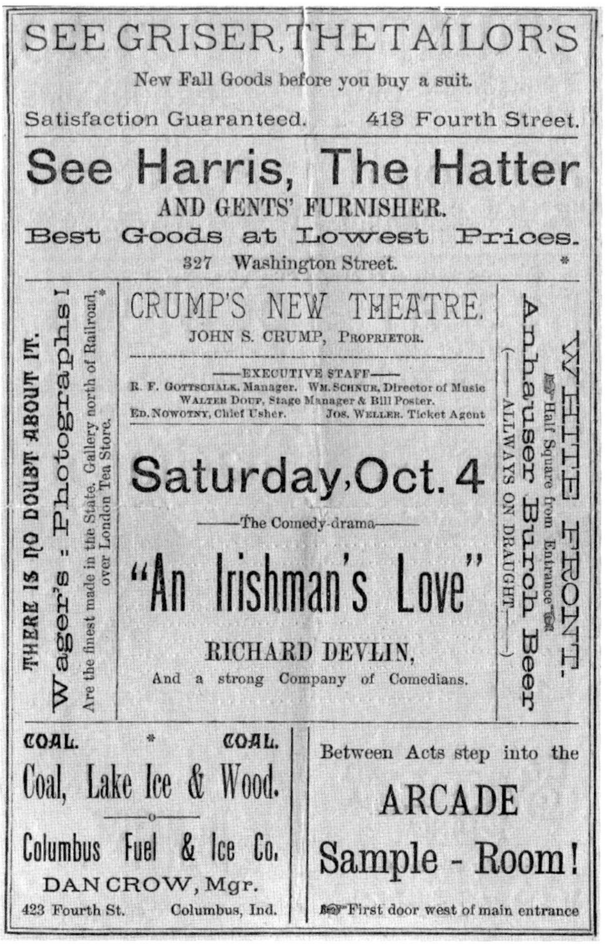
SEE GRISER, THE TAILOR'S
New Fall Goods before you buy a suit.
Satisfaction Guaranteed. 413 Fourth Street.

See Harris, The Hatter
AND GENTS' FURNISHER.
Best Goods at Lowest Prices.
327 Washington Street. *

THERE IS NO DOUBT ABOUT IT.
Wager's : Photographs!
Are the finest made in the State. Gallery north of Railroad, over London Tea Store. *

CRUMP'S NEW THEATRE.
JOHN S. CRUMP, PROPRIETOR.

—EXECUTIVE STAFF—
R. F. GOTTSCHALK, Manager. WM. SCHNUR, Director of Music
WALTER DOUP, Stage Manager & Bill Poster.
ED. NOWOTNY, Chief Usher. JOS. WELLER. Ticket Agent

Saturday, Oct. 4
—The Comedy-drama—
"An Irishman's Love"
RICHARD DEVLIN,
And a strong Company of Comedians.

WHITE FRONT.
Half Square from Entrance
Anhauser Burch Beer
(—ALWAYS ON DRAUGHT—)

COAL. * COAL.
Coal, Lake Ice & Wood.
—o—
Columbus Fuel & Ice Co.
DAN CROW, Mgr.
423 Fourth St. Columbus, Ind.

Between Acts step into the
ARCADE
Sample - Room!
First door west of main entrance

Above: The Belvedere Hotel as depicted on the back of its business card. *Courtesy of Randy Weinantz.*

Left: Crump Theatre program, 1890. *Courtesy of Randy Weinantz.*

By May 16, 1893, all of the Crump Railway cars had been replaced. New electric cars were purchased, replacing the old mule-powered cars. To power the trolley cars, John Crump had a power plant erected in back of the Belvedere Hotel. Not only would the plant provide electric to his railway, but it would also offer electric lighting for Columbus homes. John Crump's home at the northwest corner of Seventh and Mechanic (Lafayette) Streets was the first home in the city to have electric lights.

To honor John Crump's public enterprises, on May 29, 1893, the citizens of Columbus gave a testimonial honoring his achievements. It was held inside Crump's Theatre. Music and speeches lasted two hours. Music was provided by the POS of A Band, and addresses were given by Judge F.T. Ford, Elder Z.T. Sweeney and Colonel Stansifer, among others. The master of ceremonies was Professor J.A. Carnagey. John Crump was given a gold medal inlaid with nine diamonds and inscribed with the words "John S. Crump, by citizens as a token of esteem for his public enterprise, Columbus, Indiana, May 29, 1893." After the testimonial and award, Crump's Street Railway provided free rides for two hours, with bands providing music at both the new Orinoco and Maple Grove additions.

The gold medal given to John Crump by the citizens of Columbus on May 29, 1893. *Courtesy of the Bartholomew County Historical Society.*

Throughout the balance of the 1890s, Crump's Theatre offered a wide variety of entertainment. Continuous performances, an idea brought about by Benjamin Franklin Keith in 1885 that would become known as "vaudeville," were not the case at Crump's. In fact, Crump's Theatre was closed almost as often as it was open. The opera season usually began in late September/early October and ran through late April. This was the time that Crump's took advantage of any and all performances, and there were absolutely never any shows on Sundays. In fact, it was against the law to offer any type of profitable amusements on the Sabbath. When Crump's Theatre wasn't hosting professional stage performances, it was used for social activities. High school graduation ceremonies were held there. Outside capitalists that visited Columbus were brought to the Crump to impress upon them what a sophisticated, high-class theater Columbus offered. Other activities that took place consisted of performances by mediums, spiritualists and mind readers, who were quite popular entertainers of the time. As an example, on January 6, 1899, noted medium Dr. John J. Alexander performed at Crump's Theatre in front of a packed house for one night only. Tables rose and floated through the air, and flowers magically appeared from nowhere. Who wouldn't want to see something like that?

John Crump was fifty-six years old. His accomplishments reflected a forward-thinking view of civic, public and private enterprise, and his actions displayed a love for both the city of Columbus and his fellow man. John Crump served as host and guest speaker when Columbus's new city hall building was dedicated on March 26, 1895. The banquet was held at the Belvedere Hotel. Mayor Beck praised their host, proposing a toast to Mr.

Early performance inside Crump's New Theatre, 1897. *Courtesy of the Bartholomew County Historical Society.*

Crump: "Ladies and gentlemen, I propose a toast to our host! None so generous, none so enterprising as he."

In July 1899, Crump announced plans for the John S. Crump War Museum. The museum was set up inside his theater, occupying the west side of the building. John was a collector of artifacts, and with the opening of the museum, he became a curator as well. Admission to the museum was free, and Crump had chairs added for the comfort of both shoppers and war veterans alike. The centerpiece of the museum was to

Right: A photo of John Smith Crump taken between 1893 and 1898. *Courtesy of the Bartholomew County Historical Society.*

Below: Minor changes were made to the façade of the old Keith's Arcade building. A canopy was added above the entranceway to the theatre. *Courtesy of Carol Ahlbrand.*

be the "Spanish Gun," a souvenir from the Spanish-American War given to the city of Columbus by Indiana governor James Atwell Mount. (The gun would not be shipped to Columbus until June 1900, and it was first put on public display on July 4, 1900. I do not know if it was ever put on display inside Crump's museum).

Before the year 1899 was officially closed, John Crump, along with John Perry, created a public park for the city of Columbus. The park would be located in an area called Perry's Grove, a tract of wooded land north of Sixteenth Street and (at that time) bordered by Washington Street to the west and Pearl Street to the east. Perry donated the land, and John Crump had a bandstand erected. He also provided a refreshment stand and seating for summer concerts at the park.

Manager Richard Gottschalk's Crump Theatre bookings for the upcoming opera season were pretty much wrapped up by August 1899. A few of the amusements scheduled for the upcoming season were Dorothy Lewis in *Heart of the Blue Ridge*, Willard Newell in *Cyrano de Bergerac*, Marie Lamour and Frederic Murphy in *A Wise Woman: Have You Seen Smith?* and Robert Mantell in *The Dagger and the Cross*.

On December 13, 1899, the Chicago Symphony Orchestra performed to a packed house. The crowd was so immense that chairs were placed in the orchestra pit and in the aisles, with some patrons even standing to witness the performances. The stage was filled with forty-six members of the symphony, which was conducted by Adolph Rosenbecker. The *Evening Republican* reported: "It breathed fitfully the music of the spheres and a thousand and more harmonies, erotic, spiritual and sublime. The orchestra rendered music that was no less music to the untutored than it was to the musical critic, and therefore each and every number was warmly and enthusiastically applauded."

To close out the century, on December 31, 1899, a grand celebration rang throughout the entire city. Anvils were fired, bells rang, marching bands played and fireworks exploded. The last time a new year had been rung in so enthusiastically in Columbus was 1876.

1900–20

VAUDEVILLE, COMPETITION AND NEW BEGINNINGS

Merriam Webster defines "vaudeville" as "stage entertainment consisting of various acts (as performing animals, comedians or singers)." Benjamin Franklin Keith took the concept of vaudeville to a new level. He threw a bunch of different acts up on stage; let them perform continuous shows every hour, eight to ten hours a day; and charged customers a nickel to get in, making a lot of money in the process. He began a nationwide distribution chain of his B.F. Keith's Theaters in Boston at the end of the nineteenth century. In the early 1900s, there were B.F. Keith's Theaters in Kokomo, Lafayette, Terre Haute and Indianapolis.

Keith wasn't the only one to come up with this idea. While Keith worked his way west opening houses across the country, Morris Meyerfeld and Martin Beck, from San Francisco, worked their way east. Their chain of vaudeville and movie theaters was called the Orpheum.

Crump's Theatre was about to see its first real competition. On January 5, 1906, the Knights of Pythias building, also known as Castle Hall, at 416–420 Fifth Street, was dedicated. O.H. Murray and a group of investors rented out the auditorium at the rear of the building. By September 3, 1906, everything was in place, and Murray opened the Orpheum Theatre, Columbus's first vaudeville house. The Orpheum was managed by Harry Love, who also performed his own act, "The Man with the Cane," in which he danced and juggled cards. Other entertainment on opening night included Clayton Hufford singing, Ellis and Clemens and their magic act and Arthur Browning, a sad little tramp,

Crump's Theatre program/advertisement from August 6, 1900. *Courtesy of Randy Weinantz.*

who won over the hearts of the audience with his singing and dance routine. After all the singing, dancing and magic had been performed, "moving pictures" were shown on the "Orpheumoscope."

Was this the first time that moving pictures had been shown in Columbus? No. The earliest I was able to locate occurred on Saturday, November 11, 1905, with the opening of the Gem Theatre. Not much is known regarding the Gem other than it was located south of Zaharako's in the Irwin building on Washington Street. The first movie shown at the Gem was *The Moonshiners*, which played the entire week. Admission was five cents for children and ten cents for adults. There were six showings a day, as well as vaudeville performances. The Gem moved out of Joseph Irwin's building in January 1906 and disappeared altogether not too long after that.

Getting back to the Orpheum, the vaudeville shows didn't resemble the crude and vulgar shows that played in many vaudeville houses across the country or even those that played at the local Third Street Variety Theater in the 1880s. The shows at the Orpheum were clean-cut entertainment for the entire family and appealed to children of all ages. Advertisements leading up to the opening declared that only high-class modern vaudeville could be expected. Also, the Orpheum in Columbus would differ from other branch outlets in major cities in that it would not provide daily, continuous entertainment. Instead, there were shows every evening at 8:15, a matinee for ladies on Wednesday afternoons and a children's matinee at 3:00 p.m.

each Saturday. Admission was ten cents for regular seats or fifteen cents for reserved seating.

The Orpheum was half the size of Crump's Theatre, but it did have two things going for it: it offered a cheaper price and a constant schedule of amusements running a milk-route circuit. Admission into Crump's had not changed since it opened in October 1889: tickets cost twenty-five cents, fifty cents or one dollar. Crump's Theatre was much larger, but unlike the Orpheum, it did not offer weekly amusements. In fact, several weeks would sometimes go by with no production inside Crump's whatsoever. But there was one big difference between Crump's Theatre and the Orpheum: the quality of high-class entertainment. Crump's was like a bottle of fine, expensive French wine. The Orpheum was akin to a draft beer. Crump's capitalized on the larger productions of stage plays. It could accommodate companies traveling with three tons of scenery. The Orpheum could not. But there was a niche that each theater fulfilled within the community. The Orpheum was geared more to the common man, while Crump's appealed to this with a higher level of sophistication. But the Orpheum wouldn't be the only competition Crump's Theatre would face. The amusement floodgates were about to be thrown open, and Columbus was about to be awash with a new technology.

By 1907, John Crump's son, William, was managing Crump's Theatre. Richard Gottschalk, who had managed the theater as well as assisted in the operation of Crump's Railway, had been accidentally electrocuted while trying to repair one of the electric trolley cars. He was killed at the intersection of Eleventh and Washington Streets. Gottschalk was part of the Crump family, having married John Crump's daughter, Mary. On Richard's death, William took over as manager of his father's theater.

The entertainment bug must have run in the Crump family. With William managing the theater, John's other son, Charles, was managing his Palace Theater. This Palace (not to be confused with the earlier Pallas Theater) was situated inside the west end of the Belvedere Hotel.

Nickelodeons were becoming a popular form of cheap entertainment across the country, and the city of Columbus would be no stranger to this trend. On September 30, 1907, H.C. Russell, from Indianapolis, came to Columbus and opened a new place for amusements in what was Lehman's Dry Goods store at 327 Washington Street. He called his place the Theatorium.

The Theatorium offered a variety of amusements. It was not the type of place where people watched moving pictures through a viewfinder. Instead, moving pictures were projected on a screen for the entire audience to share and enjoy. There was a pianist who provided the music to what was being seen on the screen, as well as vocal accompaniment. In the case of the Theatorium, Columbus native Charlie Sewell was hired as the pianist. In addition to movies, the Theatorium also offered singing, dancing and monologues. The shows ran continuously in the afternoons and evenings. In the September 26, 1907 edition of the *Evening Republican* newspaper, H.C. Russell stated that his theater "will be the swellest of its kind in the southern part of the state."

On the evening that the Theatorium had its grand opening, Great Gay the Handcuff King was performing at the Orpheum. Two movies were also shown: *Snake Hunting* and *How Bridget's Lover Escaped*. Two blocks away on Third Street, Miss Jane Corcoran was appearing in *The Doll's House* at Crump's.

With the nickel picture shows and vaudeville making inroads into the pocketbooks of Columbus residents, John and son/manager William Crump began exploring the possibilities of such entertainment at their theater. It would seem quite logical that Crump's Theatre was beginning to feel the squeeze from its competitors. John and William were suddenly interested in vaudeville. In early January 1908, a vaudeville circuit proposal originated out of Shelbyville, Indiana. The idea was to establish a milk-route circuit running between Shelbyville, Rushville, Franklin, Columbus and Frankfort. Vaudeville shows would be hosted at select theaters one night per week. But dwelling over the possibility of vaudeville at the Crump Theatre was about as far as William or John would take the idea.

Opera houses such as Crump's and the Shelbyville Opera House had no ties to any amusement chains, as the Orpheum had. It was entirely up to the managers of such places to book all performances. If an act cancelled, it was the responsibility of the theater manager to find a replacement. If Crump's Theatre had the same opportunity of circuit bookings, it seems William's job would have been much easier. But as it was, he was solely responsible for all Crump Theatre bookings.

So, by January 1908, amusements in Columbus included Charles Crump's Palace Theatre (Third Street), the Orpheum on Fifth Street, the Theatorium on Washington Street and Crump's Theatre, all within two blocks of one another. Crump's, however, still held on tight to the reins of a higher class of entertainment, and dipping its toes into the waters of

The stage setting for a scientist's lecture at Crump's Theatre, March 8, 1908. *Courtesy of Randy Weinantz.*

vaudeville just wasn't something William (and, possibly, his father) wished to get into at the time. It was their purpose, their raison d'être, to offer such quality amusements as Jules Murry's *At Yale*, the Lyman Twins' *The Yankee Doodle Drummers*, *The Lion and the Mouse* (straight from a performance at the English Theatre in Indianapolis) and the southern-based story *Tempest and Sunshine*.

Washington Street in 1908 must have been quite a thrilling area to traverse. With the arrival of spring, downtown streets began to take on the air of an amusement park. Barkers (usually the theater managers) stood out on the sidewalk in front of the Orpheum and Theatorium, shouting to anyone within earshot. "Just beginning, just commencing, no waits, no delays. You will have to hurry if you wish seats," was manager Harry Russell's spiel from outside the Theatorium (Harry mysteriously disappeared one day, leaving in his wake several unpaid bills around Columbus). But Harry wasn't the only one barking. Kids yelled through megaphones announcing the evening's activities at the Airdome, and a man employed by the Orpheum stood at the intersection of Fifth and Washington Streets hawking the Orpheum's evening wares. Farther south on Washington, a man armed with a megaphone was trying to lure people into Charles Crump's Palace Theatre. In addition to the amusement barkers, bands played on street corners, songs of salvation

A look at the Crump Theatre auditorium prior to the 1920 remodel. The sign at the back of the balcony reads: No Shouting! No Whistling! No Stamping of Feet Allowed Here. *Courtesy of Randy Weinantz.*

were sung by church groups and, to top it all off, street vendors hawked their peanuts, popcorn, candy and other treats. Crump's Theatre was too sophisticated to add a barker into the mix.

One would think that four places of amusements would have quite satisfied any and all desires for entertainment. But four just wasn't enough—very soon, there would be two more.

The "to do or not to do" question of vaudeville that William Crump pondered over the winter months was answered in late April: Crump's Theatre would take vaudeville on a test run for one week beginning the first week in May. Instead of working with the manager of the Shelbyville Opera House, Crump turned his direction to an opera house in Greensburg, Indiana. The two would alternate their booked acts twice weekly, and if everything went well, Crump's would offer vaudeville acts during the summer months. There would also be a matinee on Wednesday and Saturday afternoons. But admission to Crump's shows wouldn't be a nickel. It would cost either ten or twenty cents to get in. The first vaudeville show at Crump's Theatre occurred on May 4, 1908. Five acts were on the bill: Franz Caesar and Company (magician), Julian and Dyer (comedy/juggling), Willard Reed and Miss Nancy St. John (musical numbers), Johnny Rowley (comedy/juggling/acrobatics) and Miss Ollie Johnson, who closed out the evening with a balancing and punching-bag bit, all while riding her bicycle. No moving pictures would be shown inside Crump's Theatre.

At the same time that Crump's was offering up its first vaudeville billing, another debut would be taking place three blocks north at a rather large lot on the west side of Washington and just south of the post office at Sixth Street. This lot was home to L.J. Lehman's Airdome Theatre, and Lehman was about to offer something unique: outdoor moving pictures. An ad in the *Evening Republican* proclaimed:

> *The motion pictures we show are unexcelled and combine the highest degree of photographic perfection with originality of subjects. We will have comedy that is humorous, scenic effects that are inspiring in their grandeur, dramatic*

An unidentified Crump Theatre stage setting, circa 1908. *Courtesy of Randy Weinantz.*

> *effects that are superb, pathos that is not maudlin, scenes of human interest to touch a responsive chord, and illusions that amaze. Our travelogue slides illustrate the world's most magnificent scenery.*

The first showing was scheduled for May 4, 1908, but due to inclement weather and a commodious amount of mud, the debut was postponed until the weather cooperated, on May 11. The first movies shown outside at the Airdome were *Collecting Post Cards*, *Durand Family at Landers*, *The French Spy*, *Shamrock* and *Famous Paintings*—all for the price of one nickel. New shows would appear each Monday, Wednesday and Friday.

I believe that the Airdome, in small-town Columbus, Indiana, should qualify as the first outdoor cinema in the United States.

Meanwhile, less than three blocks away, vaudeville was just capital at Crump's Theatre. Ticket sales were very good. Things were going so well that Crump's would offer a special show for the orphan home kids for their Saturday matinee. By all indications, the trial period of vaudeville at the theater was successful enough to warrant summertime bookings and showings (although none were advertised that summer).

With the debut of moving pictures at the Airdome Theatre, people now had five choices for movies, vaudeville or both. There was one more that would be added. Joseph L. Schwartzkopf, son of George Schwartzkopf of Schwartzkopf's Opera House fame, took the storefront at 412 Washington Street, refitted the room, bought a Motiograph model 1908 projector and opened his Lyric Theater on September 28, 1908. It was Joseph Schwartzkopf's plan to display the best quality in moving pictures. The Motiograph model 1908 was top of the line, giving a smooth steadiness in motion picture showing. Admission to the Lyric was a nickel.

Although the first movie shown at the Lyric was advertised as a "talking picture," it wasn't the first talkie to be shown in Columbus. The Orpheum had been showing talking pictures for a while. In fact, the man and lady who stood in back of the movie screen and provided the voices at the Orpheum would be doing the same at the Lyric. And Charlie Sewell would once again provide the piano music (by all indications, Charlie had been the pianist for every amusement establishment in Columbus at one time or another). The Lyric would operate continuously. It was open every evening (except Sundays) from 7:00 p.m. to 10:00 p.m., with an afternoon showing at 2:30. The first talking picture shown at the Lyric was *Crazed by Jealousy: A Romance of the West.* Talking over the picture was provided by Mr. and Mrs. Hunter and a Mr. Duncan. The trio also sang a couple of songs before the showing of the movie.

The Lyric, the Theatorium, the Orpheum, the Palace, the Airdome Theatre and Crump's Theatre all competed for a piece of the amusement pie. All were situated relatively close to each other. All with the exception of Crump's jumped on board the moving-picture fad of this period and rode it as far as they could. As vaudeville and the nickelodeons began to lose consumer interest, all but two would disappear: the Orpheum, which would become the Crystal, the American and, finally, the Rio Theater; and Crump's Theatre. But during the time that all six were a part of our downtown, it must have been quite a time.

Not much is known regarding Charles Crump's Palace Theatre on Third Street. During my research, I did not run across one advertisement for his theater, which I find somewhat strange because by this time, all theaters prominently advertised their showings. However, I did run across one interesting thing regarding Charles. He was probably the first in Columbus to show his own movies at his Palace Theatre. I call them movies, but they were actually nothing more than a slide show accompanied by music. Charles would take his camera, scout out a location, lay out a story line, either hire or choose people he knew and take his pictures. Once the pictures were taken, he took the glass plates and had them colorized. Upon getting the plates back, he laid out the story in pictures and showed them, accompanied by a selection of music, to Palace Theatre audiences. The first of Charles's movies was entitled *Playing School*. It included pictures he had taken of various Columbus school buildings and students.

On February 24, 1914, John Crump celebrated his seventy-first birthday. He was still directly involved with the operations of his Crump's Theatre. His office was inside the corner room of the Belvedere Hotel at Third and Franklin, and in the same room was his safe deposit vault and a display of Indian artifacts. By now, he had sold all of his stock holdings in the First National Bank to his brother, Frank T. Crump. He had also sold his Crump's Railway. His business efforts now turned strictly to real estate, loaning money and his theater. The front part of his theater building was bringing in a steady cash flow. There was now a barber shop on the east side and a real estate office on the west side of the entranceway, plus there was the Opera House Flats, two apartments situated on the second story.

The ever-growing popularity of moving pictures and the fact that this new medium was not being taken advantage of at his theater must have been weighing heavily on John's mind. What was happening in other Columbus theaters could not be ignored any longer. There was now stiff competition at the Crystal Theatre (formerly the Orpheum—it had changed hands), the

New Era Theatre and the Lyric Theatre, all of which offered the amusement-going public movies on a regular basis. Both the New Era and the Crystal had weathered the moving pictures mania of 1908. The Theatorium was now gone. Charles Crump's Palace Theatre was no longer in business, and "outdoor cinema" at the Airdome had vanished almost as quickly as it had started. John Crump must have realized that moving pictures were something more than just a passing fad; they were here to stay. His theater could be utilized more efficiently. Opening at the beginning of the opera season and shutting down during the summer months was a business plan that definitely needed to be addressed, which he would in the coming months.

Our history books record that the first movie reels inside Crump's Theatre were shown on May 6, 1914. But as it turns out, movie reels had been shown at Crump's prior to that date. On August 4, 1913, there was a showing of a "movie" shot by the Columbus Commercial Club. As Crump's Theatre had given vaudeville a test run in 1908, it is very likely that a similar test was done with movies. Regardless of what and when was first, this much is fact: Crump's Theatre would begin to offer regularly scheduled showings of movies in 1914.

On Thanksgiving Day 1914, Crump's Theatre showed a double feature: *When Broadway Was a Trail* and *In the Lion's Den*. These movies weren't your typical one-, two- or four-reelers that were shown constantly at the New Era and Crystal Theatres. *When Broadway Was a Trail* was a five-reel movie, running approximately seventy-five minutes, and *In the Lion's Den* was a three-reeler, clocking in at about forty-five minutes. And this would become the Crump Theatre's selling point. While opera season would still continue as shows could be booked, movies would begin to take on the more prominent role of the business model. Movies of nothing less than six reels would be shown on weeknights and Saturday nights and during Saturday matinees. Ticket prices were fixed at five and ten cents. With the theater being able to seat nine hundred people, Crump once again capitalized on quality (six- or eight-reel movies) versus quantity (two- to four-reelers). The sales concept was simple: your nickel and/or dime will go a lot further at Crump's than it will up the block. But at five- and ten-cent admissions, Crump's Theatre needed many more nickels than what was being taken in at the other box offices. Concessions weren't yet a means of bringing in more money. It was quite the opposite scenario, as Crump's Theater actually encouraged people to bring their own snacks. The bottom line was that if Crump's was going to adapt, nine hundred seats just weren't enough.

A 1914 ad for "moving pictures" at Crump's Theatre. *Courtesy of the Bartholomew County Historical Society.*

The theater John Crump had originally constructed "ten years into the future" had suddenly caught up with time. Crump's Theatre was suddenly too small. It needed to be bigger in order to hold onto its prestige "theatre" status in the community (as well as increasing profits). Crump's Theatre already offered more seating capacity than the New Era Theatre (approximately 225 to 250 seats) or the Crystal Theatre (approximately 450 to 500 seats). Both the Crystal and New Era Theatres were "landlocked" because of their locations. Any expansion of either with the purpose of accommodating two thousand people would have been extremely difficult if not impossible. But the possibility of a new theater that could rival Crump's was quite real and, most likely, a threat that could not be ignored. Two weeks before the Crump Theatre's Thanksgiving Day showings, a newly formed corporation announced its intentions of building a theater in Columbus. The intent was to build an up-to-date house that could accommodate stage plays, vaudeville and moving pictures and seat two thousand people. The interesting aspect of this is that the theater was never built. Members of the mysterious corporation were never disclosed. Had this been the final deciding factor in John Crump's decision to have his theater remodeled? Did he possibly play a role in the group's decision not to build? Alas, we will never know. Whatever role was played out during that time, one thing was certain: Crump's Theatre would be enlarged. Only John Crump would not be there on opening night.

At 9:30 on Wednesday night, January 28, 1920, John Crump, age seventy-six, died inside his Seventh and Lafayette Street home. He had suffered from a long illness, and his health had deteriorated rapidly in the days leading up to his death. The funeral was held at his home the following day. He was laid to rest in the Crump burial ground of the City Cemetery. He was buried alongside his wife, Emma, who had preceded him in death three years earlier. The Crump burial plot was originally the location of his railway trolley barn. Out of respect, his theater was closed the day after his passing.

John Crump's vision and what he tried to accomplish during his lifetime can possibly be best stated using his own words. On March 25, 1895, the dedication for Columbus's new city hall building was held in the Belvedere Hotel, with John Crump offering up the following testimonial:

> *Though the elements of progress are often complex and obscure, we may hope to unravel the tangled skein and throw some helpful light upon the subject if we look at it in three aspects common to all human life, namely, the moral, intellectual and physical. The development of this city, as all other life, inverts this order. The earliest phase is physical. A patient, systematic and untiring industry is the citizen's first virtue. To apply this force at the point of maximum efficiency requires intellectual effort. Habits of industry, the intelligent application of principles, the observation of facts in themselves and their relations to each other, the power of quick perception, which no sign, however subtle, escapes; every quality that goes to make an assured success in city life is at the same time both the cause and the effect of physical and mental growth. On the physical side, the resources are widened; on the mental, the ability to catch flying opportunity on the wing and to utilize it is sharpened. As two harmonious notes struck in*

John Smith Crump, shortly before his death. Crump was a man whose life was dedicated to his fellow man. *Courtesy of Randy Weinantz.*

> *unison on a perfectly tuned instrument will not only sound themselves, but will set a third, and this completes the accord so a legitimate development of the physical and mental life will awaken into being the moral sense that which makes the honest man what he is, the noblest work of God will make the community noble as well. Industry is power; knowledge is power, but far above and beyond both, lifting both into a higher and wider sphere of action, is the power of character.* (Columbus Herald, 1895)

John Crump strived to make Columbus a better place to live. His theater, railway, power plant and the Belvedere Hotel were the tangible reminders of what he left in his wake. Countless other acts of philanthropy were known only by himself, his closest friends, his family and those he helped.

Six days after John Crump's passing, Crump Theatre manager C.E. Rogers announced that Crump's would be remodeled according to the desires of John Crump's children, who wished to pay tribute to the wishes of their late father. Crump's Theatre was on the verge of a major change.

1920
THE FIRST REMODEL

On February 10, 1920, plans for the remodel of Crump's were hand-delivered to the Indianapolis State Industrial Board by C.E. Rogers, Robert Ruddick and William Crump. The plans were given the green light two days later. The 1920 remodel of Crump's Theatre was a massive undertaking. Rental agreements with the Clarence Howe barbershop and Columbus Real Estate were terminated, and the businesses moved on to other locations in the city. The Opera House Flats apartments on the second floor were also cleared out of any remaining tenants.

The bid for the remodel was awarded on April 2, 1920. Hege and Company secured the work with a bid of $28,600. Overall project costs were estimated at $35,000. Work on the remodel commenced ten days later. One of the more charming characteristics of Crump's Theatre would be forever lost during this reconstruction. The *Evening Republic* reported: "All of the theater from the stage to and including the front of the building will be torn away and newly built. Nothing but the side walls from the stage to the front will remain when the work is completed." That attractive, three-arched exterior that had graced Third Street for the past thirty-nine years would be forever lost, as would all the arches incorporated in the façade. Once the front was vacated, everything from the stage forward was gutted. Interior work included the addition of steel beam supports to brace the balcony. The supporting walls in the front were removed entirely, making the front one gigantic room. This area would become the mezzanine. Post supports that had been originally incorporated in the auditorium itself had made it impossible to use more than one movie projector. All were removed, part of the reason being to provide a second movie projector. The box office was relocated to the front center of the first floor and directly below the addition of the new mezzanine area on the second floor. Two exits were added on either side of the box office. The floors throughout were poured concrete, and once completed, every aspect of the interior—from the drop curtain to the carpeting—was new. In order to accommodate this massive restructuring, the theater was closed for most of the summer.

By September 1920, the new movie equipment arrived. Two new, up-to-date movie projectors and the new screen were set up. The expansion had dictated a larger screen. Dimensions of the new Minusa screen measured eighteen feet by fourteen feet. The new seats had also arrived, and workmen were busy getting them put in place and bolted to the concrete floor.

On Sunday, October 3, 1920, Crump's Theatre was open for public inspection. This gave the community a chance to see the changes firsthand and to purchase tickets for the official opening the next evening. More than five hundred people showed up to take a tour of the place. Manager Rogers hired an orchestra, and music filled the hall. The theater could

With the 1920 remodel, Crump's Theatre lost that beautiful three-arched design of the old Keith's Arcade building. Both the interior and exterior were completely remodeled from the stage to the front. *Courtesy of the Bartholomew County Historical Society.*

now accommodate two thousand plus. With the addition of the second-floor mezzanine, dances could also fill the upstairs. Those who visited that Sunday afternoon were enthusiastic. John Crump would no doubt have been proud.

Fifteen or more representatives from film companies attended Crump's grand reopening. Companies such as Pathe, the Real Art Company and Select Pictures sent floral arrangements. A line began to form an hour before the doors were opened, and by 7:00 p.m. on Monday, October 4, 1920, the house was jam-packed. More than three thousand people took part in the evening's celebration. Two movies were shown: *One Hour Before Dawn*, a mystery starring H.B. Warner and Anna Q. Nilsson, and the comedy *An Eastern Westerner*, a Hal Roach picture starring the popular Harold Lloyd.

The updated Crump Theatre was, once again, one of the finest theaters not only in Columbus but also in all of southern Indiana. Before moving on, I would like to note that John Crump did have the theater redecorated in the summer of 1903. Henry Ranje, who had worked on his father's opera house, was hired to oversee all interior design improvements. Redecorating consisted of a new drop curtain painted by Bink Schnur. New paint schemes of green, rose and gold colors filled the auditorium. Walter Doup, stage manager, updated the mechanics of moving the large scenes on and off stage. No structural changes were made to the building at the time, however.

By 1923, the sudden rush of competitors that had been born from the popularity and novelty of the nickelodeon had all disappeared. The Crump Theatre was left with one serious competitor: the American Theatre. Sometime between 1918 and 1920, F.J. Rembusch Enterprises bought the Crystal Theatre (originally the Orpheum) on Fifth Street and renamed it the American. The new owner was Frank Rembusch, who also owned the Alhambra Theatre in Shelbyville, Indiana.

Even though there were now only two places of amusements in Columbus, the American and the Crump were having a hard time making a go of it. Ticket sales were in a slump, and both were running in the red. It seemed that Columbus could no longer financially support two movie houses. In early 1923, Frank approached John Crump's heirs, who now owned the Crump, and offered to sell them the American. They weren't interested. In all probability, I doubt that any of the heirs had the hands-on experience necessary to run the business. Charles Crump's Palace Theatre lasted only a few years at the most. William Crump had managed the theater, but he was no longer around. Months after his father died, William died from an overdose of chloral. Since John's death, the children had relied on Crump manager C.E. Rogers to handle the day-to-day activities.

Since the Crump heirs were not interested in purchasing the American, Frank leased the Crump from them. On April 1, 1923, Frank took control of the Crump, signing a three-year lease. Crump manager Rogers retired, and American Theatre manager Frank Horn took over both places. Since Frank now operated both theaters, his initial intent was to offer continuous showings at the Crump six days a week while opening the American on Saturdays only, but that never happened. The Crump, however, would remain the premiere theater in Columbus.

Frank Rembusch did a number of things on acquiring the Crump. He built a larger orchestra, increasing the six-piece band to nine, and he began offering movie serials, or chapter plays, before the feature presentation. But neither of these minor adjustments could compare to what Frank instigated on August 1, 1926. The events that unfolded in the days that followed would become the single biggest controversy in the history of the Crump Theatre.

1926–29

THE FIGHT FOR SUNDAY MOVIES

In the early afternoon of Sunday, August 1, 1926, a crowd of inquisitive onlookers began to gather in front of the Crump Theatre. A rumor started the night before had drawn the curious to this Third Street location: Frank Rembusch was going to open the Crump Theatre on Sunday. But of greater importance was the fact that he was going to charge admission, and in doing so, he would be breaking an old Indiana "blue law" by operating his place of business on the Sabbath. The growing crowd wanted to see if it was true.

Indeed, it was. At approximately 2:00 p.m., Frank Rembusch, accompanied by five of his employees, opened up the Crump Theatre. Donald Wagner stepped into his ticket booth and began selling tickets. Walter Doup took the ticket stubs; Thomas Horn sat at the piano, waiting (probably anxiously) for William Norman to start up the projector; and manager Frank Horn most likely stood close by and greeted the 250 people who bought tickets. Around 2:15, the movie got underway. No sooner had the movie started when police chief George Chandler walked through the doors with a small force of police officers trailing behind. William Norman and Donald Wagner had locked themselves inside their booths. When asked by Chandler to produce a key, Rembusch balked and said he didn't have one (which he didn't). Chief Chandler then pulled out his club and smashed in the door to the projection booth. On hearing the commotion, Donald Wagner, who was busy selling tickets from inside a locked glass cage, relented, opened the door and stepped out. All six men were arrested, taken to jail and booked on a charge of desecrating the Sabbath. Bonds were fixed at $200 each. Once the bonds were paid, Rembusch and his employees went back to the Crump and ran the movie until closing time with no further police interference (you could be arrested only once a day, it seems). Incidentally, the movie chosen by Rembusch for that Sunday viewing was *The Ten Commandments* (1923).

Frank Rembusch figured there would be trouble. He had tried to open the Crump at some point prior to that Sunday, but the police were there and stopped him. This time, his attorneys, C.J. Kollmeyer and Fred Eldean, accompanied him.

The case against the six men was broken up. Frank Rembusch, Donald Wagner and William Norman appeared in court on Monday morning, August 2, 1926, along with a fair-sized crowd of Columbus citizens. Trial was set for later in the week. Frank Horn, Thomas Horn and Walter Doup would be tried at a later date.

According to the *Evening Republican*, Rembusch had this to say regarding the arrest:

> *I'll say this to the mothers of the community: from a moral standpoint, it is better for their children to be in a movie show on Sunday night than out automobile riding. We have no fight to make with anyone. We are in the entertainment business, and as the people will go some place and do something to be entertained, we feel that it is better for them to be in motion picture shows which are regulated than in a lot of other places. The people of Columbus will be entertained, and if we do not have shows here on Sunday, they will go some other place for their entertainment. We're putting our pictures up against automobile riding, the summer amusement camps, dancing, soda pop, baseball games and all the rest. There also is a commercial side to the proposition. We have been losing money in operating our two shows here, and inasmuch as the Columbus people go to other cities for their weekend amusement, we see no reason in not supplying it to them here.*

In Frank's eyes, he had good reason to be upset. He owned at least five movie houses in surrounding cities, and all of his theaters, except Columbus, were open on Sundays. To make matters worse, out of twenty-some businesses that were open that Sunday, the Crump Theatre was the only business shut down by police. To prosecuting attorney John E. Summa, that did not matter. As he saw it, it was an Indiana law. Period. And Frank Rembusch had broken the law.

The case went to trial on Thursday, August 5, 1926. It took four hours to select a jury of six men. O.B. Anderson, proprietor of a Columbus drugstore, was released after telling the court that his place of business was open on Sunday and that it would be difficult for him to render a fair decision. Potential juror John H. Cooper was released after he told the court his religious beliefs might prejudice the outcome. Once the jury was selected, it took the state forty-five minutes to present its case. By 5:30 p.m., the case went to the jury. At 10:30 p.m., the jury announced it could not reach a decision in the matter. After many tries, the votes remained split at three to three. Judge A.T. Conner released the jury and announced that the men would be retried.

This Sunday movie battle instigated by Rembusch set off a firestorm throughout Columbus and created strong public conviction on both sides. The courts were involved, as were Columbus churches. Rembusch's crusade for Sunday movies continued throughout the entire month of August. Each Sunday, Rembusch came up with something different. On August 8, he "rented" out the Crump to Indianapolis businessman Oscar Kuschner, a man of Jewish faith. Frank's defense in this instance was that this man honors the Sabbath on Saturday and not Sunday. Regardless of the day of worship, police arrived, the movie was stopped and Oscar Kuschner and his employee, Howard Cornell, were arrested. On August 15, Rembusch attempted to show a movie with the proceeds going to an "unofficial" charitable cause (money was collected for the Salvation Army, but there were none in Columbus at the time). The movie was once again halted and the men arrested. By Saturday, August 21, Prosecutor Summa was fed up and threatened to shut down the Crump, throw the lawbreakers in jail and ask for prison time. On August 22, plans to show the movie *Lightnin'* fell through when the man hired to take tickets didn't show up due to sickness. No movie was shown. To close out the month, on August 29, the crowd saw a display of large log chains padlocked across the doors of the Crump Theatre. The placard attached simply let the curious know that they could drive to surrounding towns and catch a movie (incidentally, the movie playing at the Crump the next day was *Padlocked*).

The crowd of onlookers gained in strength with each passing Sunday. If Frank wanted to get noticed, he succeeded in spades. People filled up not only the sidewalks along Third Street but also the street itself. For any passing motorists wishing to navigate that part of town, it was quite tricky.

The fight for Sunday movies was in the courts and in the news for weeks. August came to a close, and so did Frank Rembusch's attempts to show

Sunday movies at the Crump. The case against him eventually made it to circuit court, where all parties were acquitted. Frank may have lost this battle, but the war was far from over.

For the next three years, it was business as usual at the Crump. There were no further attempts on Frank's part to challenge the legal system regarding his Sunday movies crusade, and the matter was all but forgotten. By 1929, the Crump was showing movies six nights a week (continuous showings), with at least one matinee offered each weekday. The occasional vaudeville acts still cut up on stage, as well as musical entertainment. On Thursday, March 7, 1929, Gwendolyn Adams and her Petite Jazz Sweethearts Girls Band played the Crump. After an encore or two, patrons were also treated to the movie *The First Kiss* (1928), starring Fay Wray and Gary Cooper. The lineup was most likely very enjoyable and quite exciting, but something grander was taking place behind the scenes.

While the girls played and Wray and Cooper swooned folks at the Crump that Thursday evening, there was another form of entertainment going on four blocks away. The National Guard Armory at Seventh and Franklin kicked off a three-day automobile show. More than two thousand people showed up the first day alone, and the new Dodge Victory wasn't the only thing the crowd had come to see.

On Thursday, March 7, 1929, the first all-talking movies shown in Columbus were being viewed at the armory. The movies themselves were drawing as much attention and interest as the automobile—so much so that many of the men, women and children in attendance sat through the double feature twice.

Frank Rembusch was more than familiar with this new technology. According to Frank's grandson, Michael Rembusch, Frank was very "hands on," and his Alhambra Theatre in Shelbyville, Indiana, was one of the first theaters in the state strictly designed to offer movies with synchronized sound. The same day the first talking movies in Columbus were being shown at the Armory, Frank and his employees were busy setting up the new Moviephone equipment inside the Crump, and on Sunday, March 10, 1929, he took it for a test run. That day, 1,200 people took advantage of the free admission and watched two all-talking shorts. They were nothing but teasers—just enough to whet the appetite and pack the Crump the following night for the first, all-talking movies: *Redskin* (1929), starring Richard Dix, and *That Party in Person* (1929), a talkie short starring Eddie Cantor.

Two things happened that Sunday: the Crump hosted its first talking movies, and Frank's crusade to show movies on the Sabbath was reborn.

The scene that took place inside the Crump Theatre on Sunday, April 7, 1929, was reminiscent of what had transpired two and a half years earlier. At 2:00 p.m., Frank Rembusch, his son Truman (nineteen years old) and Donald Wagner (twenty-one years old) opened the Crump for business. Wagner stepped inside the ticket booth and began selling tickets. Truman secured whatever movie was to be shown, readied the projector and locked himself inside the projection booth. Frank, in the company of his attorney, Ralph H. Spaugh, and Donald Wagner's father, Charles, took their seats and waited for the inevitable to happen. At 2:30, Truman fired up the projector. A few minutes later, police chief George Chandler, accompanied by officer George Moore, entered the Crump. Officer Moore stopped Wagner from selling any more tickets. Chief Chandler approached the ground-floor projection room and demanded that Truman stop the movie. Truman refused. On Chandler's threat to break down the door, Truman relented, turned off the projector and opened the door. Frank, Truman and Wagner were arrested and taken to city hall on charges of desecrating the Sabbath. After the men were released on bond, Frank and attorney Spaugh performed a walkthrough of downtown Columbus and listed a multitude of other businesses that were open. The list was taken to Prosecutor Dobbins with demands that these merchants be arrested as well. Dobbins refused. Frank cried discrimination and persecution, noting that the Crump Theatre was the only business targeted by police.

When I spoke with Michael Rembusch about his father, Truman, he told me, "[Truman] was a frustrated attorney. I don't think he cared much about motion pictures. He was much more involved with championing the small exhibitor." This description fits Truman's father, Frank, as well. Owners and operators of movie theaters from other towns showed more than just a passing interest. They had been following the developments dating back to 1926, a few even coming to Columbus to observe the court proceedings. Whether or not Frank's crusade played a role in other theater owner's battles is not known, but they were paying attention.

Frank's renewed battle to show Sunday movies at the Crump would take a more refined approach this time. Instead of employing trickery ("renting" the Crump to a man of Jewish faith) or all-out rebelliousness (charging admission on consecutive Sundays, knowing full well that arrests would be made), he began gathering as much public support as possible. The following Sunday, April 14, 1929, he opened the Crump once again. The rain that afternoon was no deterrent in keeping away the hundreds of people who showed up. Officer Waughtel was assigned to keep an eye on things. Shortly before 2:15, manager Frank Horn stepped inside the ticket booth and hung up the "Free Admission" sign. Officer Waughtel soon left but returned occasionally throughout the afternoon and evening to ensure that no admission was being charged. A packed house watched Reginald Denny in *The Journey to Jerusalem* and an all-talking short. Five free showings were given that afternoon and evening.

In the days following the free movies, public support of Sunday movies at the Crump began to strengthen. This time around, Columbus clergymen remained concerned but were relatively quiet. There were no Sunday morning sermons denouncing the practice as there had been in 1926. Frank met with members of the city council and, possibly, members of the police committee.

By Thursday, April 18, 1929, an agreement was reached among all parties involved. There would be no further arrests or police action to close up the Crump Theatre unless complaints by individuals or organizations were made. Signed affidavits would be needed before the police would step in.

It had taken Frank Rembusch almost three years to reach this joyous conclusion. Yet there was one final question that needed to be addressed. The wrong answer to the question could possibly cause public support to change in a heartbeat. The question was asked by Columbus clergymen: would the Crump Theatre be open during Sunday evening church services? Frank assured them that it wouldn't. The theater would be dark during those hours.

On Sunday, April 21, 1929, the first "for-profit" movie, *All at Sea*, starring Karl Dane and George Arthur was shown at the Crump Theatre. The standard admission of ten, twenty-five and thirty-five cents was charged. Three showings were offered that afternoon and evening, and as Frank had promised, the Crump was closed up during evening church services. Even though there remained opposition to Sunday movies by a select group, no complaints were filed at city hall. I am sure that by Monday morning, Frank breathed a sigh of relief.

Regarding the charges of Sabbath desecration against Frank and his employees, once again, jurors were unable to reach a verdict. The case was dismissed and never retried. Thus ends the most challenging case ever to occur in Crump Theatre history.

1934–35

THE SECOND REMODEL AND THE CONTEST TO CHANGE THE THEATER'S NAME

Louis Holwager opened his Madison, Indiana Grand Opera House in 1886. This was the opera house that had impressed John Crump so much that he patterned his own theater on its design. Forty-five years later, on December 30, 1931, Holwager and his wife bought the Crump Theatre from John's heirs for $50,000. At the time of the sale, the Crump was still under lease to Rembusch Enterprises. This arrangement didn't change. There was talk of another major renovation shortly after the Holwagers bought the Crump, with estimates up to $25,000 to modernize the theater. This second major renovation of the Crump would not take place at that time, however, possibly because Frank Rembusch wasn't ready to undertake it financially. The remodel was put off.

Sometime between 1931 and 1934, Truman Rembusch, Frank's son, formed Syndicated Theaters Inc. According to Truman's son, Michael, Truman left Notre Dame University in 1928 to go to work for his father. He learned the movie theater business through hands-on experience. His first job was installing sound equipment in his father's theaters. On February 7, 1934, a ten-year lease for the Crump Theatre was formalized between Syndicated Theaters owner, Truman Rembusch, and Crump Theatre owner, Louis Holwager. The Crump's second major renovation commenced a week after signing the lease.

The Crump Theatre's sound system was at the top of the list of things that needed to be addressed. A new RCA high-fidelity sound system was installed the week after the lease was signed, and the old movie screen was

The first marquee was added during the exterior remodel of 1935 and after the contest to change the name of Crump's Theatre. *Courtesy of the Bartholomew County Historical Society.*

replaced with a new Vocalite screen. The Vocalite, actually embedded with glass beads, offered moviegoers a huge step up in watching movies. Colors were more vibrant, and it also offered much better sound penetration and clarity, as the speakers of the day were mounted directly in back. Staying in tune with the upgraded sound system, the old acoustic panels inside the theater were replaced with a product called Nu-wood, a decorative acoustic tile that came in various colors.

The remodel of 1934 took five months. The Crump stayed open all but five days. This time, all work was contained to the interior of the theater. Plush red seats were installed on the main floor and balcony, the main floor sitting seven hundred quite comfortably. Each chair on the aisle now had a light. New carpeting was laid throughout the lobby, and comfortable seating was provided. The air-conditioning system was also updated during this remodel. Black glass tiles made up the bottom of the lobby walls, and aluminum frames were mounted where the latest movie posters were displayed. By July 13, 1934, the remodel work was completed.

Although movies were now the major form of entertainment at the Crump Theatre, even as late as 1934, an occasional vaudeville act appeared onstage. On February 16 and 17, the Crump hosted a musical revue of lovely ladies. The highlight of the evening was a chorus of gorgeous beauties wrapped in cellophane. In March, Harry Berry's Sunkist Vanities appeared on the Crump stage. Days after the completion of the remodel work, Black's Animal Show, complete with midget horses, bears and many other animals, entertained theatergoers. And last but by no means least, on November 1, Doc Schneider's Texas Yodeling Cowboys entertained Crump audiences.

Another extremely popular item that caught on with moviegoers at the time was the weekend midnight shows. The young people of Columbus especially enjoyed these late-night entertainment outings.

Other than movies and vaudeville, there was also a variety of locally sponsored entertainment held at the Crump. Fashion shows gave Columbus clothing merchants such as Dell Brothers a place to show off their latest line of clothing. The newest and greatest fashion items and accessories were paraded across the stage by handpicked Columbus residents. On November 13, 1934, Alexander Davis, health and beauty expert, kicked off his three-day seminar on beauty and charm by parking a 1934 Chevrolet sedan out front (the sedan was provided by local car dealer Powell Chevrolet). Community-sponsored programs such as these were free to the public and usually held in the early morning or afternoon. The target audience was normally mothers or single women who were not employed.

As 1934 came to a close, the Crump Theatre was once again thoroughly modern and up to date. And with the Crump being the premiere movie house in Columbus, it was important to the managers and owners that they keep up with the latest and greatest in sound equipment, movie screens, projectors and other paraphernalia that made the moviegoing experience just that much better. The Crump Theatre was now forty-five years old. The theater that John Crump had built—the theater that bore his name—no longer had any ties to the Crump family. Besides updating the interior, maybe it was time to update something else: the name of the theater itself.

With the second renovation of the Crump interior now under his belt, Truman Rembusch also wanted to modernize the front exterior. In keeping in tune with the up-to-date theme, he wanted the old canopy that hung above the entrance taken down and a new marquee put up in its place. Before work commenced, though, he had an idea: what if there was a contest to update the name of the Crump Theatre, too? After all, the theater now had very little resemblance to the one John Crump had built. The exterior façade looked nothing like it did when it was first opened, and the interior had changed drastically. Maybe it was time to christen the Crump with a new moniker.

On November 6, 1934, the contest to change the name of the Crump Theatre was announced in the *Evening Republican*. The contest rules were simple: write down the new name on a piece of paper, and submit the entry. A panel of judges would determine the winner. Cash prizes totaling fifty dollars would be awarded to the top four contestants: twenty-five dollars for the first-place winner, fifteen dollars for second place and two five-dollar awards for third and fourth places. All entries had to be received at the Crump no later than 9:30 p.m., Tuesday, November 14. Winners would be chosen live on stage the following evening.

More than one thousand entries were submitted. I feel pretty comfortable in stating here that the majority of patrons who packed the Crump on the evening of November 15 came to see the winners of the contest and not the movie *Hideout*, starring Robert Montgomery and Maureen O'Sullivan. After the 7:15 showing was finished, at 8:45, the house lights came up, and Mr. C.E. Rogers took the stage.

On the Crump Theatre side, manager C.E. Rogers (back once again after a brief hiatus), owner Louis Holwager and Truman Rembusch were present. Joining them was a panel of judges consisting of Mrs. Philip R. Long, Mrs. Mary O'Bryan, Mayor H. Karl Volland, mayor-elect John L. Hosea and Walther E. Simmen. Rogers, Volland and Hosea all spoke to the crowd. Then Mr. Rogers took center stage and announced the winners. Fourth prize went to Mrs. Ralph Conrad for the name "Betsy Rogers" (which just happened to be the name of manager C.E. Rogers's daughter). Third prize was awarded to Mr. Tom Elrod for "Pioneer." Second prize was given to Mrs. Jason Lacy for "Bartholo-di." And then it was time to announce the winner. Mrs. Elsie Harris's name was called. She excitedly joined the others on stage. The judges had found her name—the "Von Ritz"—the best of all the names suggested. An enthusiastic round of applause was given to all winners.

It appeared that the Crump Theatre was about to lose its final relationship to the man who had founded it some forty-five years ago—the man who had given the city of Columbus not only its first true theater but also other public enterprises that greatly benefited many in the community. From the time the contest was announced and leading up to the selection of the winner, a question arose in the minds of the public: do we simply cast aside the name of the founder of this Columbus, Indiana landmark? Even though John Crump had been dead for fourteen years, his accomplishments had not been forgotten. Had they all been in vain? Would the final, lasting monument of his achievements rest only in the memorial that marked his grave in the city cemetery? It gives me pride to be able to answer those questions with a resounding "no." His efforts had not been in vain. There were many citizens in the community who felt that changing the name of the theater just wasn't the proper thing to do. People now referred to the theater simply as "the Crump" or "Crump's." Everyone in town knew it by that name; there was no need to follow it with the word "theater." If someone said he or she was going to the Crump, everyone knew what was meant. The contest bought forth the notion that the majority of residents felt it would be wrong to change the Crump to any other name. Although Von Ritz was the name chosen, it would never be used. Work on the Crump marquee began in early 1935, and the name "Crump" would light up that Third Street corridor for years to come.

Shortly before Christmas 1934, Sonotone equipment was installed in the Crump. This would offer deaf and hard-of-hearing patrons the opportunity to enjoy movies. It isn't known if the Crump was the first theater in the state of Indiana to install such equipment, but it was the first in the city of Columbus. A white stripe on the seat backs marked them as such for this select group of patrons. The majority of the theatergoing crowd was asked to be courteous and mindful of these seats.

By April 1935, the Crump marquee was close to completion, and something new was added that had not graced the front of the building before: electric lights. The marquee was composed of three separate parts. The illuminated "Crump" sign flashed on and off, a horizontal section of colored glass lit up and displayed the title of whatever movie was being shown and another part of colored glass showed the stars of the movie.

The final touches of the second renovation, which included a mezzanine area just off the balcony on the second floor, were almost finished. New carpeting, plants, furniture and even card tables graced this area, the color scheme rich in comfortable and appealing earth tones. Red leather chairs, vases and ferns helped decorate this area of the theater.

It should be noted here that on April 26, 1935, Irving C. Miller's Brown Skin Models, an extremely popular road show of the day, performed at the Crump for a two-night engagement. One of the cast members was thirty-nine-year-old Ethel Waters, a recording star who would move to the screen. Her notable hits were "Dinah" (1925), "Am I Blue" (1929) and "Stormy Weather," recorded two years before she appeared on the Crump Theatre stage. These three recordings would be inducted into the Grammy Hall of Fame in the late 1990s/early 2000s.

An original Crump Theatre chair, with wire rack underneath to store your hat while watching the show. The wooden seat and back do not date to 1889, but the cast-iron sides do. *Photo by David Sechrest.*

The 1920 and 1934–35 remodels of the Crump, while keeping up with the times, had overlooked one section: seating in the very back of the balcony. These few rows of seats consisted of the original chairs that had been installed in 1889. This was finally remedied and upgraded in 1937, when all the balcony seats were replaced with more comfortable cushion chairs. After the swap, the upstairs seating capacity stood at 800. The overall seating capacity of the Crump was now 1,500.

1941
THE THIRD RENOVATION OF THE CRUMP THEATRE

By 1941, there were two other movie theaters situated in downtown Columbus besides the Crump. All were within two blocks of one another. The American, at 418 Fifth Street, was now under lease of Syndicated Theaters Inc. and was christened the Rio, the theater's fourth and final name. In 1936, Syndicated Theatres opened its Mode Theatre at 315 Washington Street, designed by Chicago-based architect William Pereira. Truman Rembusch's Syndicated Theatres was solely responsible for all movie entertainment in Columbus. With one family controlling all three houses, what determined what movie played at what theater? The Crump and Mode were set up to offer first-run movies, while the Rio showed "B" movies and second-run features. If you wanted to see Gene Autry for example, you went to the Rio. The Rio was the house for "B" westerns. With the Crump being the largest of the three theaters, its size dictated which first-run movies were shown there. If a new movie was popular enough to pack the house for three consecutive nights, it played at the Crump. If the movie didn't have the drawing power to fill the Crump, it played at the Mode.

Something else occurred in 1941: the third remodel of the Crump Theatre. It is interesting to speculate why the Crump was remodeled so soon after the 1934–35 remodel. After all, only six years had gone by. Ownership did not change, and lease arrangements with Syndicated Theatres also stayed the same. The reason was, once again, modernization. Both the Rio and the Mode had Art Deco–style fronts. Both had a vitrolite front on the exterior, as well as lobbies laced with Art Deco styling. But even with the addition of

A packed house at the Crump, circa 1942. Women attend a Commercial Club meeting inside the newly remodeled Crump Theatre. *Courtesy of the Bartholomew County Historical Society.*

the Crump marquee in 1935, the front just looked old and outdated. It gave the appearance of a place your grandparents would go. It looked more like an opera house than an up-to-date, modern movie theater. In 1941, work began on remodeling the interior and exterior of the Crump.

Architect Alden Meranda did a lot of work for Truman Rembusch. Meranda came up with the Art Deco design not only for the Crump but also for other Rembusch-owned theaters in central Indiana, including the Rio, the Artcraft in Franklin and the Gibson Theatre in Batesville. Columbus architect Louis Joyner, who did an extensive study of the Crump in 1993, noted, "If you look at other Rembusch theaters, you see a lot of the same characteristics [as the Crump]."

Meranda's vitrolite front, very modern looking and extremely Art Deco, graced the Third Street corridor. The six-year-old marquee was done away with, and a more vibrant, illuminated one was put in its place. It ran horizontally across the entire width of the front. Five-foot-tall neon letters were stacked atop one another and attached to the front in a vertical

Above: The Mode Theater opened in 1936. The Art Deco front was designed by architect William Pereira. *Courtesy of the* Republic.

Right: A 1940s Rio Theatre, designed by architect Alden Meranda. The Rio's forte was "B" movies, westerns and serials. *Courtesy of the* Republic.

fashion, spelling out the word "Crump." Hundreds of incandescent bulbs pulsed on and off along the marquee, drawing attention to the title of the movie and its leading movie stars. The design has remained the same after seventy-two years.

The interior of the theater also took on the design many of us remember from our childhoods. New entrances and exits were put on either side of the ticket booth, now relocated to the outside. The circular stairway was also added. Stepping inside, there was a small inner lobby. On walking through the next set of doors, you were greeted by the man who took your ticket. The downstairs lobby was enlarged, and the main lobby restrooms were moved from the first floor to what had been the mezzanine area upstairs. On walking into the restrooms, one thought he or she had arrived in royalty. That was especially the case in the women's restroom, which was extremely spacious and finely decorated.

One of the fascinating things about this remodel, and one that every person who ever went to the Crump will remember, were the water fountains. The fountains were light activated, so if you bent over, you broke the beam of light, and a stream of water magically appeared.

It is difficult to determine whether the first snack bar was added during the 1941 remodel or the 1934 remodel. It wasn't until the early to mid-1930s that theater owners discovered that snack bars were a highly profitable source of income. Up to that time, Crump's, as well as movie theaters across the country, urged patrons to bring their own treats. Therefore, it seems logical to suggest that the first concession area inside the Crump followed the national pattern and was added during the 1934 remodel.

As a footnote, two items of interest occurred during the third Crump remodel. On October 21, 1941, Truman Rembusch purchased the Lucas property at 626 Washington Street. His plans were to build a combination movie theater/apartment complex on the site. Indianapolis architect Alden Meranda drew up a sketch of the four-story building. The theater would be located on the ground floor, and each floor above the theater would have four apartments. The theater was to be named the Esquire or the Mary K (after Rembusch's seven-year-old daughter), with construction to begin once all work at the Crump Theatre was finished. It would never be built.

The other item of interest occurred a few weeks before the Crump remodel was finished. On Friday, December 5, 1941, Louis Holwager, age seventy-five, passed away at his home in Madison, Indiana. The Crump Theatre property passed to his heirs.

Architect Alden Meranda's Art Deco front brought the Crump exterior more in line with the Rio and the Mode Theatres. *Courtesy of the Bartholomew County Historical Society.*

The main floor after completion of the 1941 remodel. *Courtesy of the Bartholomew County Historical Society.*

Seats in the "Leisure Loge," as it was referred to, cost a bit more than main-floor seats. *Courtesy of the Bartholomew County Historical Society.*

During the 1941 remodel, the Crump Theatre celebrated fifty-two years of community involvement. The building no longer resembled the one that its founder, John Crump, first opened on that rainy night of October 30, 1889. The Crump had been witness to thousands of performing actors and actresses, some good and some not so much. It first encountered vaudeville with an uneasy feeling and then provided the best that could be found. It watched quietly as silent movies grew more and more popular and listened intently as the first talkies filled its dark auditorium with the sound of voices. It learned how to adapt. It learned to listen to what its patrons demanded of it. It had weathered through the rough times and celebrated during the good. It had brought joy and laughter, tears and sorrow and all feelings in between to those who came. It was a place of respite for the weary, where for a couple hours, their problems could be cast aside.

I speak as if the Crump Theatre had a life of its own. Well, in a way, it did. Many of the people who worked behind the scenes were invisible to those who went. People went to the Crump not for the purpose of talking to the projectionist or visiting with the lady running the concession stand, but

Left: *How Green Was My Valley* (1941) was playing while work on the new marquee was in its final stages. *Courtesy of the Bartholomew County Historical Society.*

Right: The Crump closed for a short time during the 1941 remodel. *Courtesy of the Bartholomew County Historical Society.*

An updated speaker system, mounted behind the movie screen, was included in the 1941 remodel. *Courtesy of the Bartholomew County Historical Society.*

to be a part of something bigger and more wonderful that was taking place inside its walls. Everyone knew it on a first-name basis. "Let's all go to the Crump tonight." That was all that had to be said. Many residents grew up with the Crump sharing a special place in their lives. That special sentiment would be shared by thousands more over the years to come and would last as long as the Crump Theatre continued to be a member of the community.

1950–70
NOTHING EVER QUITE AS GOOD

The Crump's Most Popular Era

Throughout World War II, the Crump Theatre chipped in and did its part. War bonds and stamps were sold in the lobby. The war tax slightly increased the cost of admission, bumping up the price a penny or two. The Crump offered special matinees for defense workers each Tuesday and Friday at noon. In this time before television, newsreels helped to keep patrons informed of what was going on overseas. For a short time, all late-night shows were cancelled because of an imposed curfew.

Roughly eight years after the 1941 Crump remodel and facelift, in March 1949, Truman Rembusch bought the Crump Theatre property from the Holwager heirs. He paid $150,000 for both the theatre and an adjoining building/property to its east and had it put in the names of his children. In addition to owning and/or operating all of the movie theaters in Columbus, Rembusch and Syndicated Theaters also owned WCSI, a local radio station, whose offices moved into the building adjoining the Crump Theatre later that year.

In 1945, the war came to a close. A prosperous new decade lie ahead for the city of Columbus. As the 1940s gave way to the 1950s, the city of Columbus experienced a tremendous growth in business and personal enterprise. New jobs drew more people to the city. The first suburbs and strip malls began popping up on the outskirts of town. In 1949, the first television station, Indianapolis-based WFBM-TV (Channel 6), broadcast into Columbus homes. And more stations would follow. In 1950, the second "supermarket" in the city, Standard Grocery, opened

Above: Restrooms were relocated to the second floor during the 1941 remodel. *Courtesy of the Bartholomew County Historical Society.*

Right: A glance down the aisle of the Crump Theatre. Art Deco–designed covers hang where box seats were once located. *Courtesy of the Bartholomew County Historical Society.*

Many gimmicks were used to get moviegoers inside the Crump—this is one from 1948. *Courtesy of the Bartholomew County Historical Society.*

at the corner of Ninth and Washington Streets. In August 1950, the Columbus Drive-In (one mile north on 31-A) invited people to "come as you are" and enjoy a double feature from the comfort of your own automobile. By the mid-'50s, teenagers discovered a newfound freedom that none of their predecessors had ever experienced. And through all the growth and change, the Crump Theatre held on to its status as the premier theater in Columbus.

However, through all the changes, one thing remained constant: the Crump Theatre projectionists. Michael Rembusch recalls:

> *The great story about the Crump is the Crippen brothers. If you saw a movie exhibited in Columbus, Indiana, from after the war until the 1970s, it was exhibited by one of the Crippen brothers. Bill was the projectionist at the Crump, and Herschel was the projectionist at the Columbus Drive-In. Their other brother, Nate, was the relief operator. It was one of the Crippen brothers that ran every show in Columbus.*

According to Herschel Crippen's son, Herschel Jr., his father started working at the Crump in 1937. Herschel Jr. recalls:

> *Mom and Dad got married in 1939. Dad was working at the Crump at the time, and they gave him a raise from seven dollars to nine dollars a week. He didn't strictly work the Crump. He did maintenance work and was projectionist at all the theaters, and in the 1950s, he would have been spending most of his time out at the Drive-In. By then, Bill was pretty much the projectionist at the Crump. Mom was the cashier occasionally at the Crump and the Drive-In. She got robbed one night while working at the Crump, and she retired after that. That was enough of that stuff. Dad used to borrow my BB gun and go down to the Crump and shoot pigeons flying around in there.*

Herschel retired in the late 1970s after spending more than forty years working at Columbus theaters, and I doubt there was anyone who knew the inside of the Crump better than he did.

If I had to pick a time when the Crump Theatre was most popular, it would be during the 1950s and '60s. I write these words with some prejudice, as this was the time of my youth. It was my time, and the Crump was an important part of my childhood. I remember what it was like to go to the Crump during this time. I remember how, on certain nights, the line of people waiting to get in stretched its way along the Third Street sidewalk to Franklin Street and then turned south and sometimes ran as far south as Second Street. It was an incredible time to grow up in Columbus, and it was an incredible time to go to the Crump.

This is the time period in the history of the Crump Theatre that many reading this book will remember the most. Each and every one of us has our own personal memories of this Crump Theatre. And we hold these memories close to our hearts. We cherish them as much as photos of loved ones we keep tucked away in family picture albums. The Crump Theatre was a part of our families, just as the houses where we grew up and the grade schools we attended. There are hundreds of thousands of memories of the Crump. Each is unique and separate, but at the same time, all are collectively kept and stored inside. They are the common bond that ties all of us together, for any mention of the word "Crump" will automatically trigger a story of a happy time. It's the commonality we all share and one we can all relate to.

Some of my fondest memories of the Crump Theatre are of summer and the Thursday morning movies sponsored by the Junior Citizens League and Thompson's Dairy. Both a boy's and girl's Schwinn bicycle was given away each Thursday morning. Maybe you were there. Maybe we watched *The Time Machine*, *Journey to the Seventh Planet* and *House on Haunted Hill* together

The downstairs lobby was a gathering place for friends to meet and buy snacks at the concession stand. *Courtesy of the Bartholomew County Historical Society.*

Above: WCSI's birthday party, 1948. *Courtesy of the Bartholomew County Historical Society*.

Left: Many ladies fondly remember the Crump Theatre ladies' room. Walking in made one feel as though she were royalty. *Courtesy of the Bartholomew County Historical Society*.

on those Thursday mornings in the summer of 1962. And if you are the girl who found a Necco wafer in your hair that I spit out during a frightful scene in *House on Haunted Hill*, I apologize profusely.

I will leave any further memories of the Crump Theatre and my youth for another time and place. In closing out this part of the narrative, I will ask for a moment of silence. This is your time of reflection—a time to recall those days of yesteryear and the special Crump Theatre memories you hold dear to your heart.

1970–2013
DETERIORATION, RUMORS OF DEMOLITION AND A NEWFOUND INTEREST

As the 1960s gave way to the 1970s, things at the Crump began to change. A downward spiral began to take hold. As the city of Columbus expanded ever outward, so did the shopping habits of its people. It was all happening in the suburbs. Downtown merchants were having a go of trying to compete and, in many cases, joined their competition in parts of town that had been farmland less than fifteen years earlier. In 1968, Columbus Cinemas, a two-screen venue, opened in Columbus Center. By 1974, Courthouse Cinemas opened less than a block from the Crump. The Rio Theatre on Fifth Street, which had certainly seen better days, became a community arts playhouse. And to round out movie entertainment in and around Columbus, the Drive-In was still going strong. In addition to local competition now threatening the Crump were the drive-ins and movie theaters in Greenwood and Indianapolis. Work on I-65, connecting Columbus to Indianapolis, was finished by the early 1970s, and more and more people were venturing out of town in search of entertainment. We were now a mobile society.

The Crump Theatre simply could no longer compete. Shopping, travel and entertainment habits of the people had changed, and no update—no matter how grand—or modernization of the movie house itself could bring back the customer count to the numbers of ten years ago. To add insult to injury, on Sunday, December 17, 1978, the Crump Theatre came very close to being destroyed. The building next door that had once housed the WCSI offices caught fire early that Sunday morning.

The fire was contained to that building, but the Crump would not go unscathed. Approximately $30,000 in smoke damage was sustained. The Crump closed up so that necessary repairs could be made. Many historical artifacts dating to the theater's early days were lost. Early movie posters and bills that had been put away for safekeeping were so damaged by smoke that they were tossed in the trash.

Throughout the late 1970s and on into the 1980s, the Crump continued along this path of deterioration, slow decay and drop-off in business. It was becoming more difficult to get any top-grossing movies booked. Individual movie theaters in Columbus now had to bid on the latest blockbusters. In a 1987 *Evening Republican* newspaper interview with Fred Crews, Crump Theatre manager, Crews said, "We just haven't gotten too many top shows here. They're going to the other two theaters in town." And if the other two movies houses weren't getting them, the movies the Crump did get were two weeks behind their premiere showings in Indianapolis movie houses. By then, it was too late. Any potentially interested Columbus patrons had already traveled to Indianapolis to watch the movies.

The look of the lobby remained the same throughout the 1960s and '70s. *Courtesy of the Bartholomew County Historical Society.*

Due to competition and bidding wars, attendance at the Crump had dropped off considerably in 1981. *Courtesy of the Bartholomew County Historical Society.*

By this time, the Crump Theatre was owned by Margrat Inc. and leased to Truman Rembusch's Syndicated Theaters. Margrat had been formed in 1945 by Truman, initially as a trust fund, and was named after his children: Mary Kay, Gracie and Truman Jr. At some point, Truman Jr.'s interest was bought out by his sisters.

In April 1987, Margrat dropped a bomb on Columbus residents. The company requested a bid from Columbus-based Shultz Excavating Company to provide a quote for the demolition of the Crump Theatre building. This caught everyone in Columbus, especially Crump manager Fred Crews, by total surprise. "My bosses haven't said a word to me. The first I heard of it was when you called Friday. Just bang—all of a sudden," Fred told *Evening Republican* reporter Joseph Gill.

The news was quite a shock to the community. The Crump had been a downtown fixture for close to a century. Even though things weren't great, no one would have ever imagined that things had gotten so bad that there was suddenly, and totally out of the blue, the possibility that the theater would be demolished.

Fortunately for the Crump, one Columbus resident was paying close attention to what was going on. In 1989, Vernon Jewell stepped forward. Vernon explains what happened next:

The Rembusch family owned it. They had leased it to Kerasotes. Kerasotes also had the theater out on the east side of town. They had that one, and they had the one at the Commons, so they were operating all three. I was county commissioner at the time, and the commissioner's chambers were right across the street [from the Crump]. *We had Monday meetings, and I'd sit in there and look at that old Crump building. I was sitting in another meeting with the city, and Terry Darno, who was planning director for the city at the time, made the comment that she heard that there was a good possibility that the Crump Theatre would be demolished. And so I was just sitting and thought, "Man, that's kind of sad, because the old building has been around for so many years and has such a good history." I thought about it for awhile, and while talking to my son-in-law, who was a realtor, I said to Milo, "I heard that the Crump Theatre might be torn down. I really hate to hear that. I wonder if it's for sale." Milo asked if I wanted him to find out, and I said, "Yeah, I'd be interested. I might be interested in buying it depending on the price." So he went ahead and came back and said that a family out of Franklin owns it—the old original Rembusch family. So Milo asked if I wanted him to try and contact them, and I said yes but that I won't give over x amount of dollars. So I went to Florida and came back, and Milo said, "Hey Vernon—I bought that building while you were gone."*

So that's how I bought that thing. I bought it while I was on vacation and didn't even know it at the time. I'm not sure that anybody even knew that I bought it.

After I bought it, I thought, "What am I going to do with it?" I only bought it to try and make sure that it was not going to be demolished. And then I thought, "Well, I'll do my part in trying to salvage the building." So after I bought it, I went to Trudie Underwood [now Trudie Schoettmer], *who was the operator there* [with Kerasotes], *and she helped me run it. I rented the building to Kerasotes. It was operating as a movie theater the whole time I owned it.*

After I bought it, the word got out, and then I had several people that wanted to start a dinner theater or had something they wanted to start promoting. I was never interested in doing that. The needs of that building were so great, but all I wanted to do was just save the building until I could sell it to somebody who I thought was going to try to restore it. But Trudie was the one. If it hadn't been for her, I probably wouldn't have been able to hang onto the building as long as I did. She helped a lot on some of the things that needed to be done.

During the time I had it, I was approached by John Dornbush from Irwin Management, and he asked me what my intentions were. I told him the only reason I had the Crump building was because I hated to think of it being torn down. He said there might be a group that might be interested in buying it, so I met with John Dornbush, Fred Myers from Arvin, maybe Randy Tucker and Hutch Schumaker. There were probably six or seven of us there. And they told me there was a possibility that they might be interested in buying the Crump. Later, they came back and told me they definitely wanted to buy it. There was a group from Arvin, Cummins and Irwin Management that was interested. They wanted to explore the possibilities of what could be done with it. They were getting ready to have a 1992 celebration of Columbus discovering America, and that's when they were trying to complete Mill Race Park. They asked me if I would hold onto it until after the celebration.

They asked during that meeting if I wanted a contract, and I looked around the room and said, "If I can't trust you guys to live up to your word, then who can I trust?" So I told them that yes, I would hold onto it. I told them, "When you get ready to buy, let me know, and I'll be here." 1992 and 1993 came and went, and I heard nothing back from them. So I contacted them. When I called them back, I said, "Hey guys, I've been hanging onto the Crump. I've had some buyers that have wanted it, but I would not do it because I was afraid that it would not turn into something nice. I think it's time for you guys to step up and do it." I can't remember what year I sold it [it was 1994], *but I called them up and said, "Hey guys, the 1992 celebration is over with. Where do we stand on this Crump building?" And they stepped up and bought it.*

Vernon also shared something else that took place around the time he sold the Crump building:

But also, to go back, after they [the Columbus Capital Foundation] *had decided that they were going to purchase it, they went to the city. In fact, I think a city member was involved in that meeting. They had it worked out with the city and all the groups that they thought might be interested in using it…they would turn it into a performing arts theater. The Columbus Philharmonic had concerns about the size of the stage and whether it would be big enough to put a whole orchestra up there. There were some from the Arts Guild that were concerned about the proscenium arch not being wide enough. And all of them had these concerns as to what needed to be done to fit their requirements of what their needs would be. So the city brought in an architect. I forget what the architect's name was, but he had done some work here in Columbus. I met with him and the Miller family, who were also down there at the time, and the architect came back and said, "We can take the back off." The city said they would close up the alley behind it, so that would give them the additional space going to the south. They could close the alley to the west of it. Irwin Management owned that vacant lot to the east, and they said they would give that to the Crump. That would leave the main part of the theater there, but from the proscenium arch on back, it could all be redone. That would give them all that room to the east, west and south in order to make that work. So it was kind of a done deal for the city. Then they went back to some of these groups, and my understanding is that some of the people involved in the Philharmonic said they didn't want to share. Then some of the others said they didn't want to share either. They wanted their own building. So finally it came down to, "Hey, if these people want their own building, let them build their own building." The money was there. It could have been done at that time. But they could not get the cooperation of the rest of the people to use it. But*

Since the 1941 remodel, this mural has been a fixture inside the Crump lobby. The artist is unknown. *Courtesy of the Bartholomew County Historical Society.*

> *there was interest at Cummins, Arvin and Irwin Management. They were willing. They had the money, the cooperation of the city, an architect and everything they needed to redo that building. And it fell through because all of these people wanted their own facilities. The commitment was there to turn it into something really nice.*

One really can't blame the different organizations for wanting their own places. With the amount of money it would take to renovate the Crump to fulfill any one of their needs, a new structure could be erected from the ground up. "That story has been around since the 1970s," Columbus architect Louis Joyner told me. "Everybody's wanted to use it, but no one has had the vision to make it work."

The group that bought the Crump Theatre from Vernon Jewell was the Columbus Capital Foundation. Hutch Schumaker explains, "The Columbus Capital Foundation was put together around the time we bought the Crump. It started for various reasons. Irwin Management helped fund putting it together. Its charter was to save buildings of significance or pieces of property of significance for the community for future use."

By the time the Columbus Capital Foundation bought the Crump Theatre in May 1994, wear and tear and a general lack of maintenance on the building had taken its toll. While the building may have appeared healthy from that Third Street corridor, it was quite the opposite once you stepped inside, and that might partly explain why Margrat had sought bids for demolition. I'll let Hutch Schumaker pick up where Vernon left off:

> *This Crump situation came up, and we thought it would be a great place for the Columbus Capital Foundation. So the Miller family donated the funds to the CCF to purchase the Crump from Vernon Jewell. Will* [Miller] *and I went in there and said, "Wow, now what have we done? What do we have here?" Part of the roof had caved in, and the boiler was completely shot. At that point, it was pretty close to the wrecking ball.*
>
> *It would appear on the face of it, to most people, that it was in such bad shape that bringing it back up to a sustainable level was a daunting task. So we took a look at it, and I thought, "Well, we need to stabilize it and then figure out what to do." So then we started the analysis of what needed to be done. The primary goal in mind was to stabilize the building so that it could sit unused or used until someone came up with an idea for its ultimate best use. We had the boiler re-tubed, but the main thing was rebuilding the big truss that was holding up the roof. It had caved in, and there was water*

> *coming in. I had nine fifty-five-gallon drums in the balcony with siphon hoses going out to the alley.*
>
> *So we finally raised enough money locally to have the roof completely done. That was tearing off the old roof completely and rebuilding that truss. So then we re-tubed the existing boiler. I looked into buying a new boiler, but they were incredibly expensive. Baker Boiler out of Indianapolis said they could re-tube this thing. They re-tubed the boiler, and then it was back up—and while not as efficient as a modern boiler, it operates perfectly. So the heating and air conditioning was fixed, and the roof was secure.*

The group that also helped raise funds for this work was Save the Crump, a grassroots effort founded by Hutch Schumaker. Many people in the community, as well as local foundations, contributed and raised approximately $150,000, plus there was a matching $50,000 grant from the Indiana Department of Natural Resources Division of Historic Preservation. Save the Crump volunteers also took on the massive job of cleaning all the garbage out of the Crump. Hutch continued:

> *As we moved along this path, it got to the point where the Crump was going to be completed to where it had been twenty-five years prior. We did a lot of rewiring. Unfortunately, it was nothing that went, "Wow, all new seats!" It was all infrastructure, and it was all needed. Then, later on, we actually did the marquee. And I went out and raised $25,000 and got another $25,000 matching grant from the DNR and had the marquee completely restored. We got new ballasts and new electrical panels. So, there you are.*

(Hutch also mentioned that he was able to track down a source for the vitrolite tiles that adorn the front exterior. At the present time, they are in storage. Once the time is right, the broken panels will be replaced, and the Crump Theatre will look as fresh as it did after the 1941 remodel.)

From the time that the Columbus Capital Foundation purchased the Crump in 1994 up through the completion of all the structural work Hutch mentioned, it took five years to get the Crump Theatre structurally sound. The year 1995, in particular, was a terrible year for the Crump Theatre. On January 31, 1995, the Crump Theatre's lease with Kerasotes expired. The company did not renew it. To make matters worse, the boiler broke down, and the Crump was closed. This occurred shortly after the Columbus Capital Foundation took charge of the theater and in the same year that Schumaker formed the Save the Crump campaign. By the end of 1995,

The interior and exterior remodel work was completed by early 1942. *Courtesy of the Bartholomew County Historical Society.*

the Crump Theatre reopened just before Christmas. In celebration of the reopening, the movie *Miracle On 34th Street* was shown. Special posters were made up with the declaration of it being a "Miracle on 3rd Street" in honor of the theater being open once again. The Crump would remain open for another two years as a dollar venue before being shut down again in 1997 so that the roof and marquee could be replaced. In 1997, the Crump Theatre, the premier movie theater the city of Columbus had known for the majority of its life, would never again reopen as a movie theater.

For the most part, it was the first time in eighty-four years that the movie screen went blank. The main feature, in quiet finality, had come to the end. The hero did not ride off into the sunset. There was no applause from an enthusiastic packed house. The end came more along the line of, "If you are the last person leaving, please turn off the lights on your way out." This shining jewel that once lit up Third Street had simply outlived its usefulness as a movie house.

Throughout the late 1990s and early 2000s, the Crump was open on a very limited basis. This time period in the theater's history was filled with work on the building's infrastructure. Its needs were overwhelming. Rovene Quigley assumed the job of Crump Theatre manager as an unpaid volunteer in September 2003. Rovene's first involvement with the theater, however, dates back to 1972. As a member of the Driftwood Valley Arts Council (now the Columbus Area Arts Council), she proposed that the DVAC buy the Crump for the purpose of turning it into a community

Let's all go to the snack bar! It is uncertain whether this photograph was taken in the Crump, the Mode or the Rio. *Courtesy of the Bartholomew County Historical Society.*

arts center. In the late 1980s, she heard that the Crump was for sale and spoke with Michael Rembusch about buying it. Things would not progress beyond the talking stage.

In the early 2000s, Rovene took a portion of the Crump funds and had the old electrical system updated. The work included all new electrical panels and some rewiring. She played an instrumental role in getting local contractors to donate labor hours to further the necessary repairs and updates that the building's infrastructure desperately needed. "I worked the jail inmates. They spent the whole winter cleaning this place," Rovene told me during a May 28, 2013 interview at the Crump. Rovene did run a few movies at the Crump, but with little success. But Rovene's true strength was in the hosting of live music events, and she developed a strong bond with the young people in Columbus while doing so. She recalls, "When I first started here, I said, 'I think I'll have a yard sale.' I talked to Casey Cole, who had a band, and I told him to bring his band down and make some noise while we're having this rummage sale. So they did. I mean, 150 kids showed up. So I talked to Casey, and I said, 'Let's try a night and get some more bands together and see what happens.' We were rolling for a while." Personally, this is Rovene's most important role. Through her efforts, a younger demographic was made aware of two things: the naked beauty of the Crump, and its challenges. The Crump had once again become a place where memories could be made. As those of us who fondly remember the Crump of our younger years, so too will this new group of young people. To me, this is the key to any future the Crump Theatre might have. It is extremely important for a younger demographic to have the opportunity to build their own memories inside this special place. If our children are not aware of it, it will no longer serve a purpose. It will no longer have a history. It will most definitely be overlooked and forgotten. There must be that relationship between the two in order for it to survive. And because of this, I believe that Rovene has played an extremely important role in championing the Crump Theatre's future.

There have been two memorable events at the Crump Theatre while Rovene has been in charge. In the early 2000s, there was a special showing of a movie based on the Shackleton Antarctic expedition. This was a special fundraising effort, with tickets costing $200. The other event was the John Mellencamp concert on September 23, 2008, which was made into a television special. The performance was filmed for the BIO channel. It was entitled *Homeward Bound: John Mellencamp* and was first shown on December 11, 2008.

A special gathering for Cummins Engine Company employees. *Courtesy of the Bartholomew County Historical Society.*

Another source of income that Rovene helped to generate, and one that no one would have dreamed of twenty or even ten years ago, was the sudden interest in the paranormal aspects of the Crump Theatre. During our meeting, Rovene showed me her Crump booking calendar, and every weekend into August was booked solid by ghost-hunter groups wanting to explore the theater. Many groups have preceded the ones I saw marked on her calendar that afternoon.

Crump Theatre ghost stories date back as far as my youth (the 1950s/'60s) and even earlier than that. One of the stories involves a distraught lover who died by jumping from the balcony. Another concerns an actor who hung himself below the stage area. When these stories first originated, I do not know. During my research, I did not uncover anyone who ever committed suicide inside the building. The closest I came was a news story dating back to April 3, 1908. Reece Williams, a tenor traveling with the Donnelly and Hatfield Minstrels, fell asleep on a cot high above the stage in the fly gallery. He rolled over and fell some thirty feet to the stage below. At first, those who found Williams thought he was dead. When they discovered he was still alive, a doctor was sent for. Williams was taken to A.J. Banker's Mercy Hospital. He had incurred

It was a very special evening for me to see the title of this book and my name on the Crump Theatre marquee. *Courtesy of Bob Anderson, Stillframes Photography.*

a fractured hip. He missed that evening's performance, but he was still with us. Is it possible that this was the starting point for future, greatly embellished ghost stories? Your guess is as good as mine.

In 1979, Ed Sullivan was hired as the first full-time executive director of Columbus's Heritage Fund, a foundation set up in 1976 for the purpose of financially helping the community. During Ed's tenure, the first feasibility study on the Crump Theatre was undertaken. As Ed explains:

> *That's when the Heritage Fund was just beginning. In the early 1980s, we were thinking about using the Crump as a project orientation. We would then raise money related to that, and at the same time, we would build an endowment. The foundation took it on as a singular project. We took great pains to really examine the Crump. We wanted to resurrect it for the community, if that was possible, as a multipurpose performance center. But to make a long story short, we went through it all and tried to estimate what it would cost to renovate it, but the limitations with the alley that runs behind it doesn't give you a chance to expand it. It was landlocked, so we decided it couldn't work. It wasn't worth resurrecting just as a movie theater. So given what it would cost and the fact that you really couldn't expand it, we just didn't think it was worth the effort.*

Over the past forty years, there have been nine separate and unique feasibility studies conducted on the Crump Theatre. There are many reasons why any of the past feasibility studies were unsuccessful in determining an eventual use for the Crump Theatre. Renovation costs and funding are two reasons that kept any particular study from going any further than they did.

In June 2013, funding for the tenth feasibility study was approved by the Columbus Redevelopment Commission. Getting to this point was no small undertaking. In April 2012, a Crump Theatre Six Sigma project team was created. Its purpose was to use the Six Sigma methods used by manufacturers, apply the same principles to the Crump Theatre and explore options that could possibly make the Crump Theatre self-sustaining. The Crump project roadmap would follow the DMAIC structure: Define the problem, Measure and collect data, Analyze the data to determine relationships and find out what exactly had caused prior (feasibility study) failures, Improve the process used this go-around and Control the variables so that any path to failure can be corrected beforehand.

The Crump Theatre marquee lights up the Third Street corridor, bringing back memories of an earlier time. *Courtesy of Gary Scroggins Photography.*

For the first time ever, the Crump Theatre was analyzed using this statistical control process. Henry Malm, Six Sigma Black Belt at Cummins Engine Company, explains:

> *One of Cummins' qualities is to help the community. We started the Crump project in April of last year* [2012]. *There is a lot of reading that you have to do to determine what has already been done with the Crump Theatre's past projects (i.e. feasibility studies). It took a lot of people from Columbus who know about the Crump. We gather a lot of information about what other people did. We gather demographic information, details and numbers, and that helps us to create a roadmap of the big picture. This is where we are going. We are then able to dice it into bits and pieces so that team members can take ownership of certain parts. Then we all bring it together as a team.*

I have always associated Six Sigma control with manufacturing processes. To be honest, this is the first time I'd ever heard of such an analytical method being used for such an intangible product as the Crump Theatre. I was intrigued.

Henry continued:

> *On the manufacturing side, we might be measuring the diameter of widgets. In the case of the Crump Theatre, for example, you can think of a widget as trying to reduce cost. We look at all the variables that make up the cost and ask, "How can we reduce the cost of each and all of these variables?" It's the same concept as manufacturing.*

The team effort that went into this study was a remarkable undertaking. As an example, each team member was assigned a prior feasibility study. They followed each one through to its end. Henry recalled:

> *We had team members go in and read the various studies and then summarize all key points we are looking for, such as what the objective of the that project was, what the outcome was and the names of the people that participated. There were criteria that we identified. What could have been done better? What went wrong? What caused this part to fail? After constructing everything, there is a complete deconstruction of everything that went wrong and an attempt to understand the individual factors that caused things to go wrong. We try to understand the mitigation strategies for the next time and try to improve it using Six Sigma.*

When I asked Henry if there was one common denominator in all the prior Crump Theatre feasibility studies that had brought about a stopping point, he said:

> *One thing that jumped out to anyone who read through all those reports was the element of financial planning that was missing in most of the studies. The idea of what they wanted the Crump to be was there, but the numbers backing it up weren't. If we invest "x" number of dollars into the building, how do you make it self-sustaining? Now, from all the reports that we read, the idea was that they wanted the Crump to be self-sustaining, but there were no numbers backing the plan. We spent all of the money renovating, but how are we going to make sure that it brings in money to fund the place, pay for the people who work there and still be able to at least break even. That was the one thing that was generally missing.*

It all boils down to this: each unique feasibility study of the past had its own specific reasons why it did not progress to the next level. I feel that it's important to note that results of any of the prior studies were not the fault of any organization or individual. The time devoted and the focus at those various times simply employed different methods. And to Henry Malm and the Six Sigma team, it was important to understand all that had transpired before. It was important to understand where the Crump had been in order to move forward.

The Crump Theatre Six Sigma project team released its findings in early 2013. The team followed a carefully outlined and constructed methodology in reaching its conclusions and recommendations. Past data was analyzed, movie theaters in Bloomington and Franklin were toured, surveys were conducted and funding options for the Crump were explored. Project costs and financial models were drawn up. Based on the data, the group's conclusions consisted of five bullet items: 1) the need for a public relations campaign; 2) the desire for the Crump Theatre to be a performing arts center; 3) the fact that potential patrons preferred live entertainment such as theater, dance and concerts; 4) the fact that both public and private funding for the Crump was possible; and 5) the fact that citizens preferred using public money to renovate the Crump.

In addition to its findings, something else occurred that would greatly benefit any future plans regarding the Crump Theatre. As an added boost, it was learned in late 2012 that an area of downtown was awarded the prestigious designation of "Indiana Cultural District" by the Indiana Arts Commission. The Crump Theatre just happens to fall within this designated area.

With the Six Sigma team report and the feasibility study approved, it was time to bring hands-on experience into the mix. The redevelopment commission approved funding to hire the Lafayette, Indiana firm of Jones and Phillips Associates Inc. to conduct the latest Crump Theatre feasibility study. Its results should be released sometime between October and December 2013.

When I met with Hutch Schumaker earlier this year, he said something to me that really clicked—"the stars being in the proper alignment" was how he put it. Is it possible that, after numerous attempts at doing something with the Crump Theatre, that those stars Hutch mentioned are beginning to align themselves properly? It seems quite possible. With the establishment of the Indiana Cultural District by the IAC, it can only provide more momentum to any future plans. Add to this exciting mix Mayor Kristen Brown's

"Advance: A Strategic Plan For Columbus," as well as other initiatives currently underway in the city, and the current time and those stars could not be brighter. Jayne Farber, project consultant with the Columbus Arts District, says, "We have a facilities development and preservation team. We want to develop facilities in town that will enhance art and culture because we now have an Arts District. And we want to preserve some of the facilities we already have, such as the Crump. This is the team that I chair, and under this comes the Crump initiative." What Jayne is referring to is one of the recommended projects in the 2013 Columbus Arts District Strategic Plan: the Crump Theatre Feasibility Study and Renovations Plan. "The mayor said we have to decide what to do with the Crump," adds Jayne. "It cannot stay as it is because it continues to fall into disrepair, and the funds that were raised and set aside from the Save the Crump initiative are almost gone. Something has to happen."

In the *Republic* newspaper article "Crump Getting Fresh Review," dated June 19, 2013, it was noted that, indeed, those Save the Crump funds are extremely close to running out. Approximately $3,000 is all that remains in the fund, and it is quite likely that if something is not done soon, the Crump Theatre will be forced to close up by the coming winter. Things always look darkest before the dawn, don't they? Even with the prospect of a proper alignment of the stars, the Crump could be in for a bumpy ride this coming winter.

So, where does all of this leave us? Is the Crump Theatre actually worth saving, or are we doing nothing more than clinging onto it because of some nostalgic memory from happier days? After devoting many months to the researching and writing of this book, I believe you know what my own personal answer to that question is. I believe we must find a way to make it fit into not only any current revitalization efforts but more importantly, it must fit into our heritage. Of all the opera houses and theaters of our past, the Crump Theatre is the last one standing. It is our final physical brick-and-mortar link to our cultural arts beginnings. Does this single fact not have any weight in our fast-paced world of today? Have we become so indifferent and nonchalant about it all that we are blind to its significance? For the sake of myself and others, I truly hope not.

As I see things, the Crump Theatre desperately needs a champion. When I met with Henry Malm, I asked him what a Crump Champion is. He answered that it was *someone who can definitely advocate its cause. If I think of it in the sense of Six Sigma, I see the Champion as what I will call the process owner. You do the work, and once the work is done, you hand it over to somebody who is part of the day-to-day operations to ensure that the process is kept alive. It is someone who will keep it going. In my mind, that is who a Crump Champion is. It would be someone who has the leverage to push back. Let's say there is an idea that we no longer want the Crump. The Crump Champion would be someone who would step up and say, "I disagree. I see it differently, and these are the reasons why." The Crump Champion should be able to address the issue constructively and in a civil manner. It would be someone who has the ability to change people's minds. Having money helps, but if that would be the only thing you had, would that make someone a Crump Champion? I would probably say otherwise. But yes, having money doesn't hurt.*

All of us can play an active role in championing the Crump Theatre. This is my own personal effort to do exactly that. It is my hope that this book will give you a refreshed understanding, as well as a newfound appreciation, of our Crump Theatre heritage. The future is exciting. I cannot think of another time in the past twenty-five years when the Crump situation has looked more promising.

It has been a long journey. Hopefully, there will be something wonderful awaiting us all at the journey's end.

Appendix

A TIMELINE OF EVENTS

October 21, 1872
Francis J. Crump opens his opera house at Fourth and Washington.

October 18, 1873
F.J. Crump's Opera House is destroyed by an early morning blaze.

October 18, 1873
In the wake of the destruction of F.J. Crump's Opera House, J.G. Schwartzkopf opens his Germania on Jackson Street.

April 23, 1874
F.J. Crump will not rebuild his opera house.

April 15, 1875
McCormack and Sweeney make preparations to build a theater on Mrs. Young's corner (southwest corner of Fifth and Washington Streets).

April 27, 1875
George P. Bissell arranges conversion of the McEwen Block into a hotel.

June 24, 1875
Colonel John A. Keith moves his law firm from the Keith Arcade building to the second floor of Keith's hardware store at the southeast corner of Third and Washington.

October 29, 1875
McCormack and Sweeney's Pallas Theater at Fifth and Washington is dedicated.

December 17, 1875
The Bissell Hotel opens.

February 20, 1879
The Pallas Theater is destroyed by fire.

March 10, 1880
Schwartzkopf plans to remodel the Germania (aka Schwartzkopf's Opera House).

May 4, 1880
The Third Street Variety Theater opens.

May 18, 1880
McCormack and Sweeney will not rebuild the Pallas Theater and build the St. Denis Hotel instead.

November 28, 1880
Schwartzkopf's Opera House is refitted.

February 25, 1881
Duffy, Condon, Irwin and Hogue announce a new opera house to be situated at Sixth and Washington.

March 10, 1881
Commercial Row (F.J. Crump's block) to be remodeled. (Commercial Row was located across from the courthouse—what we know as the A. Tross building.)

March 16, 1881
New Theater will not be built by Duffy, Condon, Irwin and Hogue. Another unnamed capitalist intends to build a theater (the unnamed person might have been F.J. Crump).

April 29, 1881
The St. Denis Hotel holds its grand opening.

April 30, 1881
Francis Jefferson Crump dies. The line of admirers who follow the funeral wagon to the Crump Homestead (present-day Mead Village) is over one mile long.

1882–88
John Crump inherits Commercial Row property from his father and rebuilds and opens his first theater on the second floor.

December 3, 1888
Colonel John A. Keith is recommitted to the Indianapolis Insane Asylum.

December 31, 1888
Advertisements for J.S. Crump's Theatre and New Years Eve Performances appear in the local newspapers.

January 28, 1889
The Keith property is auctioned off. John Crump buys Keith's Arcade for $6,000.

March 8, 1889
John Crump and Charles Sparrell travel to Madison, Indiana, to tour Louis Holwager's Grand Opera House. Crump is so impressed that he decides to pattern his new theater after the opera house.

March 20, 1889
John Crump buys the adjoining lot next to Keith's Arcade from Fred Donner.

April 22, 1889
Bids received for the building of John Crump's theater are opened. Keller and Brockman are awarded the contract.

October 30, 1889
J.S. Crump's New Theatre is opened during a downpour. It is called the finest theater in southern Indiana and is Columbus's first true Opera House.

SEPTEMBER 15, 1890
J.S. Crump's Railway, Columbus's first mass transit system, is opened.

1891
John Crump purchases the Bissell Hotel property. During the remodel, a tunnel is dug underneath Third Street, connecting his Belvedere Hotel to the theater.

DECEMBER 1, 1891
Belvedere Hotel opens. More than two hundred people attend the Grand Ball.

MAY 16, 1893
J.S. Crump's railway replaces the mule-powered trolley cars with electric cars.

MAY 29, 1893
Citizens of Columbus honor John Crump at a special testimonial given in his benefit inside the Crump Theatre.

1899
Perry's Grove (including present-day Donner Park) is donated to the city as a public park by John Perry. John Crump has a bandstand, seating and a concession stand erected for the city.

JUNE–AUGUST 1903
Crump's Theatre is redecorated.

NOVEMBER 11, 1905
The Gem Theatre opens and shows the first "moving pictures" in Columbus.

SEPTEMBER 3, 1906
The Orpheum Theatre, Columbus's first vaudeville house, opens.

1908
Columbus nickelodeons gain in popularity, and there are now five theaters within four blocks of Crump's: Charles Crump's Palace Theatre, the Orpheum (Fifth Street), the Theatorium (327 Washington Street), the Lyric Theatre (412 Washington Street) and the Airdome, just south of Sixth and Washington.

May 11, 1908
The Airdome begins showing outdoor movies. It is very possible that the Airdome was the first open-air cinema in the United States.

September 28, 1908
Joseph L. Schwartzkopf opens the Lyric Theater at 412 Washington Street.

August 4, 1913
The first movie reels are shown at the Crump Theatre.

January 28, 1920
John Crump dies at his home on Lafayette Avenue.

February 10, 1920
The first Crump Theatre renovation begins. John's heirs follow his wishes for the remodel and update. New movie projectors and movie screen are installed. The original Keith Arcade façade is done away with. The remodel opens up the interior, accommodating two thousand people.

October 4, 1920
Crump Theatre reopens.

April 1, 1923
Frank J. Rembusch leases the Crump Theatre.

August 1, 1926
Frank Rembusch and five of his employees are arrested for desecration of the Sabbath for showing movies at the Crump on Sunday. This sets off a firestorm throughout the city. The battle would continue throughout the month of August.

August 8, 1926
Rembusch "rents" the Crump to Oscar Kuschner of Indianapolis. Kuschner is Jewish. Rembusch's defense is that Kuschner honors the Sabbath on Saturday and should not be held to this Indiana "blue law." Kuschner and his employee Howard Cornell are arrested and taken to jail.

AUGUST 15, 1926
Rembusch attempts to open the Crump under the guise of donating the money to charity. Again, the movie is halted by police, and Rembusch is arrested.

SEPTEMBER 1926
Rembusch is acquitted of all charges and makes no further attempts at showing Sunday movies.

MARCH 7, 1929
The first "all-talking" movie is shown in Columbus at the National Guard Armory at Seventh and Franklin Streets.

MARCH 10, 1929
Rembusch opens the Crump on Sunday (with free admission) to show off the new projectors and sound system. The first all-talking movie is shown at the Crump.

APRIL 7, 1929
Frank Rembusch renews his fight to show Sunday movies at the Crump. The theater is shut down by police. Frank, his son Truman and Donald Wagner are arrested and taken to jail.

APRIL 18, 1929
An agreement is reached between Rembusch, the police and all parties involved in his crusade to show Sunday movies. The Crump will close during church services.

APRIL 21, 1929
The first "for-profit" movies are shown on Sunday at the Crump.

DECEMBER 30, 1930
Louis Holwager buys the Crump. The lease with Rembusch is not affected.

FEBRUARY 7, 1934
Truman Rembusch's Syndicated Theatres acquires the rental lease of the Crump.

February 14, 1934
The second major renovation gets under way, with specific plans to update the sound system and movie screen. New seats and carpeting are also installed.

November 6, 1934
The contest to change the name of the Crump is announced.

November 15, 1934
Four contest winners are announced. Mrs. Elsie Harris wins first prize (twenty-five dollars) with her suggestion of the Von Ritz. (The name would never be used.)

April 1935
The new three-piece marquee is close to completion, and the exterior offers something new: electric lights.

April 26, 1935
Ethel Waters performs on the Crump Theatre stage.

1937
Original seats dating to 1889 are removed from the last few rows in the balcony and replaced with more comfortable cushion-type chairs.

1941
The third remodel is started. The vitrolite front and a new marquee are added. New entrances and exits were installed, as was the circular stairway inside the lobby. The main lobby restrooms were relocated to the second floor.

October 21, 1941
Truman Rembusch buys the Lucas property at 626 Washington Street. His intentions are to build a movie theater/apartment complex. An Indianapolis architect sketches out what the building will look like. (The complex is never built.)

December 5, 1941
Louis Holwager dies. The Crump passes to his heirs.

March 1949
Truman Rembusch's Syndicated Theatres buys the Crump from Louis Holwager's heirs for $150,000.

August 1950
The Columbus Drive-In opens. Syndicated Theaters controls all four movies establishments in Columbus.

1950s/1960s
The Crump Theatre reaches its peak in popularity.

December 17, 1978
The Crump sustains smoke damage from a fire next door. Many historical artifacts are beyond saving.

April 1987
Margrat (a trust fund set up by Truman for his children, and which now owns the Crump) seek bids for the demolition of the Crump Theatre.

1989
Vernon Jewell buys the Crump with the sole purpose of saving it from the wrecking ball.

1994
The Columbus Capital Foundation buys the Crump from Vernon Jewell. President Hutch Schumaker becomes the Crump Champion and organizes the Save the Crump campaign with the purpose of raising funds to stabilize the building.

1995
Save the Crump kicks into high gear to raise money for structural repairs.

2001–02
The marquee and vitrolite front are restored.

September 23, 2008
A John Mellencamp concert at the Crump is filmed by the BIO channel and later released as a television special.

2008

Ghost-hunting groups begin to explore paranormal aspects inside the theater.

April 2012

The Cummins Six Sigma team is organized. Its purpose is to determine whether the Crump can become self-sustaining.

Late 2012

Downtown Columbus is awarded the designation of "Indiana Cultural District" by the IAC. The Crump falls within its boundaries.

July 15, 2013

The tenth Crump Theatre feasibility study begins. Jones and Phillips Associates Inc. of Lafayette, Indiana, undertake the viability study.

BIBLIOGRAPHY

Due to the lack of firsthand accounts and available resources on this subject matter, early editions of the *Republic* newspaper (1872–89) proved invaluable in the writing of this book and, in many cases, were the only resources available.

Columbus Herald. March 26, 1895, 4.
Columbus Republican. "No Opera House." April 23, 1874, 4.
———. October 17, 1872, 4.
———. January 7, 1873, 4.
———. October 23, 1873, 4.
———. January 29, 1874, 4.
Daily Evening Republican. November 25, 1879, 4.
Evening Republican. "Crump's to Be Enlarged." April 2, 1920, 1.
———. "John S. Crump as Benefactor of Columbus." October 5, 1889, 4.
———. "Sunday Movies Result in 6 Arrests." August 2, 1926, 3.
———. "A Word to the Public." October 8, 1889, 4.
———. February 28, 1881, 4.
———. May 2, 1881, 4.
———. February 14, 1882, 4.
———. April 15, 1889, 4.
———. October 29, 1889, 4.
———. December 31, 1899, 4.
———. April 29, 1908, 6.
———. April 13, 1987, 12.
———. April 13, 1987, 1.

INDEX

ABOUT THE AUTHOR

David Sechrest grew up in Columbus, Indiana. Some of his fondest childhood memories are of the Crump Theatre and walking to the theater from East Columbus along the railroad tracks. His passion and love for Columbus history began with a book his parents gave him for Christmas in 1997. In 2001, David moved back to his hometown after being away for thirty-one years. On his return, he created the Historic Columbus Indiana website and forum. Initially created as nothing more than a nostalgic look back at the Columbus of his youth, he soon found himself wanting to learn more about the people and places that helped shape the city. In 2005, he created Historic Columbus Celebration Day, a day set aside to honor the heritage of Columbus, Indiana. On April 14, 2007, Mayor Fred Armstrong proclaimed the day David Sechrest Day.

In May 2003, David's appendix ruptured, nearly taking his life and seriously affecting his overall health. He continues to be involved in Columbus history, but on a limited basis due to health concerns. While he is limited by physical boundaries, his passion for the past is as strong as ever. David plans to keep exploring the heritage of his hometown. He hopes to write another book one day.